presence of mind
only consciousness can discover itself as consciousness
undefinable concepts: consciousness, thinking, attention
consciousness is identical at any moment with its contents
consciousness can contain only one content at a given moment
process — thinking, willing FROM perceiving, representing
    (making mental pictures) feeling
what we observe is NORMAL always the past

TO

HEALTHY

FROM
NORMAL
TO
HEALTHY

Paths to the Liberation of Consciousness

GEORG KÜHLEWIND

translated by Michael Lipson

LINDISFARNE PRESS

This book is a translation of
VOM NORMALEN ZUM GESUNDEN, WEGE ZUR BEFREIUNG
DES ERKRANKTEN BEWUSSTSEINS by Georg Kuhlewind,
published by Verlag Freies Geistesleben GmbH, Stuttgart.

© 1983 Verlag Freiesgeistesleben GmbH, Stuttgart

This edition © 1988 The Lindisfarne Press

Published by the Lindisfarne Press,
RR 4 Box 94 A-1
Hudson, NY 12534

Printed in United States of America
10 9 8 7 6 5 4 3

designed by Judith Lerner

Library of Congress Cataloging-in-Publication Data

Kühlewind, Georg, 1924–
[Vom Normalen zum Gesunden. English]
From normal to healthy : paths to the liberation of consciousness
Georg Kühlewind ; translated by Michael Lipson.
p.   cm.
Translation of: Vom Normalen zum Gesunden.
ISBN 0-940262-10-X
1. Anthroposophy.   2. Consciousness.   I. Title.
BP596.C65K8413 1988
299'.935—dc19   88-2998
CIP

Contents

Foreword

PLEASE READ!

"DON'T I have enough problems already? What with my job, my family, my whole life . . . don't I have enough to worry about? Recession, inflation, the energy crisis, pollution . . . and now I'm supposed to worry about my consciousness? Isn't that really more for philosophers, psychologists, epistemologists, and folks like that? Are you trying to tell me that my consciousness is sick?"

Dear reader, I agree with you completely. But first consider the results of two simple experiments. I am convinced, you see, that all our troubles in "the world" and at home are caused in fact both by today's consciousness in general and by our own personal consciousnesses in particular.

For the first experiment, let me introduce a magic genie. After reading *The 1,001 Nights* I freed him from his bottle and he promised to grant me a wish. And because he owes me the work, here's what I'll have him do. First, clean up the pollution in the environment. Air, water, farmland, woodland, I want everything turned back to the way it was in, say, the year 1750, the year of Bach's death. Second, fill up the oil reservoirs, restore the mineral deposits (tin, lead, manganese, and so on) to their former levels in the same year. Third, do away with inflation and put wages and prices back to 1960 levels.

All this by tomorrow morning. He can do it easily, but when he hears about it, he'll just grin.

The question is, you see, what *next*? A week later, a year later, what will happen? We all know only too well: sooner or later everything will become just as bad as it is today. In other words, if the mentality, the consciousness of humanity doesn't change, then my genie's efforts will do us no good. "Okay," you may reply, "then there's something wrong with other people's consciousness, but mine is perfectly healthy. If it were up to me I'd make sure that things didn't fall apart again."

But no, even you and I are no exception. We all suffer from the same disease. It goes without saying that if your consciousness were healthy, you would be in control of it, the master of your consciousness. But are you? Has your consciousness never played you false? Have you never done anything that you later regretted?

Here then is another experiment. It should cause you no problem, if you're functioning healthily, to concentrate on a given theme, for instance, the necktie you're wearing, for three minutes without wavering. If you're not wearing one, then just pick any other uninteresting object. Try it out— three minutes of thinking about the tie and nothing else.

Well now, and how did you end up in Greenland? It seems as if you're not altogether master of your consciousness after all. And you're not alone. You share this weakness with all the professors, politicians, and other very practical people who, so it seems, have brought about the current situation in our world, our civilization. If none of them can even control their own consciousness, then it's possible that much of what they do and say comes not from presence of mind but from . . .

I believe that our central problem is that we do not know what or who a human being really is. We lack this knowledge because we have no valid picture of the human *word*, no image of human language, of words in general. This is why we have such trouble with words, why we hit upon the right word so rarely. Everything we do to, for, and against each other is speech of some kind, or ought to be. Yet we are interested in anything but words, these very words by means of which we do everything else. Because we don't know what words are, we don't know what humans are. And, not knowing who we are, we don't know what would be good or

8

healthy for us. Obviously, we cannot rely on our instincts here. Is it so surprising then that things go wrong? Besides, we are too complacent. We think, I'm clever and good enough, pretty much just as I am, to solve my problems and the world's problems too. I don't have to go to extraordinary lengths. But great artists have to practice for many hours a day, and we—perhaps not the greatest virtuosi in questions of cognition and morality—how much practice time do we devote to the general art of being human?

I can already hear you saying, "Two thirds of the world goes hungry, nuclear war threatens continually, there's an economic crisis, and you want to waste precious time and energy on this kind of airy speculation? How can you justify that *morally*?"

This is how I see it. All the dangers of war, starvation, and overproduction that you mention were not caused by *my* kind of airy speculation. On the contrary, all of that was caused and tolerated by the practical people. Maybe, just maybe, it would have been better if we had not listened to them in the first place. Maybe the world's perils are there precisely because the practical types, the world in general, has exercised its moral and cognitive faculties too little, has let them stay undeveloped.

Besides, your moral considerations about wasting your time and your energy would be more appropriate if you brought them up at the movies or the football stadium, or when you were playing cards. The world goes hungry, and you watch spy movies and soft porn?

Now, I think we can really begin. First we'll take stock, and try to explain phenomenologically what our consciousness contains. Then we'll examine the general symptoms of the diseased consciousness of today. After that, a little psychology to make comprehensible the remedies that are described in the following chapter. Then we'll discuss an introduction to consciousness exercises for those who wish to develop their consciousness beyond the point of simple health. Finally, there will be a glance at human freedom.

FROM
NORMAL
TO
HEALTHY

1

INVENTORY

Preliminaries

What do we find in *consciousness?* Don't ask me what consciousness is. I couldn't explain it to you if you didn't already know. In other words, every attempt to explain it presupposes that you have already had some experience of it. This, then, is our first conclusion: *only consciousness can discover itself as consciousness.* It has to see itself, and no explanation suffices to create the understanding if consciousness has not already experienced itself.

What do we find, what does consciousness find, in consciousness? Now, right now, at this moment (we hope) *thinking*. But don't ask me what thinking is. I can't explain that to you either; at best I can point it out, I can indicate it: what you're doing right now, that's it. Consciousness must see itself, discover itself as thinking. Now, if you'll pardon my asking, when was the last time you had a new thought? Think about it. If you're quick-witted you might say, "Right now I'm thinking something new by realizing that I only rarely think any new thoughts. But aside from that (you may have to admit) I can't remember when a new thought occurred to me."

13

Then what are we doing all day? Having thoughts, finished thought forms, is not thinking—or it is only thinking to the extent that finished thoughts are joined to one another by the *activity* of thinking. And even this joining together is not always thinking. It proceeds without any logic or thinking at all, in which case it is called association. It was association that distracted you from your necktie.

Most thoughts encountered by an adult are already familiar. For a small child, who is only just "learning" to think and speak (how can he learn, if he can't yet think?), all thoughts are new. Everything else within consciousness is discovered and described by thinking, by the thinking *attention*. But don't ask me what attention is. As with consciousness and thinking, I can't tell you. There are many such undefinable concepts. Remember that to define one word, I generally need at least three others. If I want to define these, then I need another nine, and so on. (Thomas Aquinas was already aware of this. Today it is generally forgotten.) Some concepts and words in the natural sciences *can* be defined, but only by relying on others that remain undefined. These latter terms are always the most fundamental concepts, such as Being, Space, Time, that is, the categories.

Attention in adults is always *thinking* attention. Although it is itself a phenomenon of consciousness, it can also be directed toward other phenomena in consciousness. This poses a new problem. Are there two phenomena in consciousness at once, attention and its object? Or are there two consciousnesses, one directed toward the phenomenon and another directed toward the first consciousness? First we must correct a conception implicit in the expression "in consciousness." This is the notion that consciousness is a vessel into which various contents can be poured. Consciousness is always the consciousness of its contents, that is, it is identical at any moment with its contents. There is no empty consciousness—the feeling of emptiness is itself a content of consciousness. The experience of emptiness can really be had only when we make a shift between different levels of consciousness. It should be obvious too that consciousness can contain only one object, only one content, at a given moment. The kind of divided consciousness or divided attention that we need to drive a car is really a rapid shift among many objects and contents. This realization makes the problem trickier: how can consciousness assess its own phenomena? The idea of two consciousnesses will have to be dropped immediately, otherwise we would have to ask, who saw and counted the two consciousnesses? There would have to be a third one. Further examination leads to surprising results: any psychological phenomenon that becomes conscious for our thinking attention is always already there in consciousness, always the result of a process—thinking, perceiving, representing (making mental pictures)—that was not itself consciously experienced. What we can observe in consciousness is always the past, never a process in the present; not even when our own activity is necessary for the process. No, we experience nothing *in* thinking or *of* thinking itself: we sleep through the thinking and find ourselves wide awake facing a *past thought*. It works the same way with perceiving and with the formation of mental pictures.

All this may seem surprising. It is as if a bird flew from limb to limb of a tree and we did not see it in flight, but only when it alighted on a branch. In consciousness, likewise, we always find the already thought, the already perceived. Because we can hardly conceive of thoughts and images arising otherwise than from a process of consciousness, ours is a consciousness of the past, conscious of its *own* past. Thus we are justified in calling normal consciousness a *past consciousness*. But we must not forget that this consciousness is capable of noticing its own past character. And so we ask, how is this possible?

You will object, rightly, that up until now we have only considered thinking. Consciousness also includes, for example, mental pictures, feeling, willing, and perceiving.

Mental pictures or representations work in the same way as thinking: they are the remembered images of perception, which we can call into consciousness through a concept or thought. We can also form an imagined picture from remembered perceptual elements. We can direct our attention *autonomously* to mental pictures just as we could with regard to thinking and perceiving. By autonomously I mean "in accordance with our conscious will." By "just as we could" I mean that the autonomy is limited, as we noticed in the example of the necktie exercise (see Foreword). Similar distractions can occur during perception.

In relation to our *feelings,* however, we are not so autonomous as in relation to thinking, representing, or perceiving. On the contrary, it is the feelings themselves that seem autonomous. Everyone is familiar with the power moods have and how hard it is to escape when a feeling takes over. A feeling enters the mind like a foreign invasion. We get to know it from the *outside;* we do not live into it from *within* as with a thought, which reveals itself to us entirely. Feelings have a greater power over us: they arise without our participation and once there we have a hard time removing them despite our own wishes. I can think about anything I choose, but I cannot feel a given feeling at will—otherwise life would be much easier!

When I meet a friend we ask each other, "How are things going?" But this question refers not so much to objective circumstances as to the mood these circumstances have evoked, and so it means more nearly, "Are you feeling good about things?"

In thinking we can improvise, as long as we are really thinking, that is, thinking something new (even if this happens only rarely). We cannot know in advance what we will think. If we knew, we would have already thought it. Innumerable new thoughts can arise. Our feeling life is different: we cannot improvise here, because we cannot bring a given feeling into consciousness at will. And then, there is not normally an unlimited range of possible feelings; the palette is quite limited—it goes from "good for me" to "bad for me," with "boredom" in the middle. With some effort we can forge new concepts, but is it even possible to have a new feeling? When was the last time you had a new feeling?

I can examine a thought the moment after it has arisen. I

have to wait for the surge of a feeling to pass off before I can observe the feeling. In the midst of experiencing it I am rarely able to call up my own attention. The waves of feeling carry me along and generally there is no unmoved center, no lighthouse in me, so to speak, from which to observe the panorama of the waves.

If the everyday life of feeling can be observed afterward, after it has calmed down, like a barely comprehensible perception, the normal life of the will cannot be observed at all. I can observe the goal of a willed activity, which is a mental picture or a thought. After focusing on this, the will takes over and completes the activity. We know of no "empty" will devoid of clear objects. After the willed activity has taken place, we can observe the result. But even then the will itself remains unconscious or superconscious, even when it seems to be *my* will, which I feel I am using by my own free initiative. The act of will remains "dark" in this way whether I do something because of external stimulus or out of desire.

Because of this dark aspect of the will, it would be meaningless to ask, "When was the last time you had a new willed impulse?" because the question would really have to refer to the will's motivation in thought. "When was the last time you had a new thought and also willed it?"

Within the realm of conscious experience, it is perception that seems most *given,* least willed. Yet it is certainly not enough to simply open your eyes in order to see. Anyone can confirm this by remembering his or her own childhood behavior at school. Children can look at their teachers with big eyes and follow their movements, with their ears wide open (since they cannot be closed) so as to hear the teacher's voice, and yet not hear or see anything. Then if the teacher asks them a question, the children have no idea what was being talked about. Every teacher is familiar with those big eyes, and the characteristic facial expression of the dreamer.

According to physics and physiology, children must have seen and heard everything said to them: the light rays or photons reached the eyes and the airwaves reached the eardrum in the ear, where they set in motion a chain of physical

and chemical reactions. These in turn initiated further processes in the nerve cells, and nothing prevented them from
reaching the brain in just the right way to cause seeing and
hearing. What was missing? "Attention," we say, "the children were not paying attention." What were they doing then?
They were dreaming, having a fantasy.

All this physiology, physics, and chemistry, was not sufficient for perception to take place. Attention has no physiological or physical correlative, and teachers have no thought
of physiology when they say, "You there, pay attention!" So
perception is not simply given after all.

Besides attention, which can be willfully withheld through
an effort of *concentration,* something else is necessary in
order to perceive *something.* We need to have a concept for
what is to be perceived. This concept can be already present
within us, or it can arise at the moment of perception, but
without it we cannot perceive *"that."* Without the concept
"house," no one sees a house. You can see walls, windows,
a chimney—if you have concepts for them. As a rule, we see
only what we have concepts for. We always perceive *something.* If we ask, what is perceived, then the answer is always
a concept.

Perception simply does not take place unless accompanied
by attention and concepts. These latter do not originate in
perceiving—we are ourselves the attention, and concepts
arise through thought intuitions. To be sure, the perceptual
world provides us with questions which must be there in
order for concepts to form: a child with severely damaged
perceptual apparatus will form concepts with difficulty or
hardly at all.

It seems as though our review of the inventory of consciousness has given us three kinds of conscious contents: in
thinking, finished thought pictures and also that free capacity
to think by which we form new thoughts and concepts; in
the life of feeling, only finished feeling forms, apparently,
with no possibility of creating new feelings; and in the life of
the will, a willing capacity that changes form according to
whether it wills an already existing thought concept or

whether it gives to a new intuition the power of realizing itself. In the life of perception and mental pictures we encounter both finished, ready-made contents and new ones.

First Ranking

It is apparent that for our inventory of consciousness we used thinking, or, more exactly, observation through thinking. This faculty explained itself to us, as well as explaining perception and feeling. If we did not have this thinking observation (if, for instance, we had only perceiving), then we would not even know that we were perceiving. We notice perception only thanks to the capacity we have for stepping back, by means of thinking, from the act of perception. In fact, from the act of seeing alone we would never guess that we see through our eyes, because healthy eyes give no clue to their own existence. It is thinking alone that lets us know the eyes play a role in seeing. Thinking prompts us to make the experiment of closing or covering our eyes and then draws the conclusion that we use our eyes to see. Uncautious thinkers—of whom there are a great number—draw the conclusion that it is the eye that sees. But we have already seen (without eyes) that this is not the case.

We seldom experience thinking in its pure form. Only when we make a great effort to think logically and scientifically do we do so, and even then we are not always successful in keeping out other activities. These other activities, feelings, associations, and moods, get mixed into our thoughts. What we normally call thinking is mostly not thinking at all. The other activities of the mind—to what extent they are truly active is an open question—are similarly heterogeneous. Feeling, for example, is always combined with mental pictures; perception contains traces of thoughts, mental pictures, and even will impulses. We have seen that the attention, which is autonomous in principle, is still greatly limited by distracting associations. In both thinking and perceiving we are tempted to wander. This phenomenon can suggest further insights.

In these cases, when the attention is led astray, it does not go to sleep or become foggy. It retains its sharpness and clarity, while unwanted objects and themes enter its field of vision. These are often as sharp and clearly defined as the originally intended object of thought, or even clearer. A power independent of our will pushes them into the focus of attention; it is not the attention that chooses them. That these unwanted contents appear for the most part sharply outlined, finished, and already formed, can aid us in one of the most important discoveries in the observation of the life of the mind.

We met such finished forms during the first step of the inventory. In the realm of thinking, we found on the one hand finished thought forms, and on the other hand the capacity to think freely by which we can form new thoughts and concepts. In the realm of feeling it is harder to find something similarly unformed that might be regarded as a *capacity*. When you see a "No Smoking" sign, for example, you don't need to cudgel your brains to know what it means. When you read the sentence, "The question of the voluntary nature of an action is therefore not a question as to its cause," you are forced to really think. But if by any chance you were a philosopher familiar with the field of ethics, then the sentence would hardly give you more trouble than "No Smoking." In the case of the philosopher much less *attention* must be brought to bear in order to understand the sentence. The process of understanding is more automatic. Although "No Smoking" is a phrase from our common language and the first time we understood the phrase we called on our common human capacity for thinking, it later became a part of the system of consciousness by which we *react*, with no active understanding or thought. In order to obey the sign we need to pay attention less and less: the phrase has been separated from the autonomous understanding of the attention.

Obviously, this kind of automatism only occurs with regard to *finished* thought forms. *New* thoughts must always be worked out through active attention. On the other hand, it still takes a certain minimum of reading or thinking attention to understand automatisms of thought: the sign means nothing to someone who cannot read at all, unless he recognizes it merely by the external form of the letters. But it is just the same, or nearly so, for someone who has seen and read the sign many times.

In the realm of feelings, such automatisms form much more readily and become even more independent, that is, more independent of the person's will, because the appearance of a feeling occurs utterly without the activity of the subject, and in fact it often appears against his will and contrary to his intention. Wishes, desires, and will impulses can attach themselves automatically to feelings. The appearance of automatisms, which in the realm of thought contents seems alien or inappropriate, counts as the normal course of events in feeling. Finished thought forms or mental pictures are often bound up with feeling forms, and this *finished world* has, because of its feeling component, a great degree of independence over the consciously willing subject that we have located in the active attention. From this finished area there come the associations, distractions, daydreams, irrational fears, modes of behavior, and psychological habits which often have biological effects—the so-called complexes, specific, biographically conditioned sensitivities, and patterns of reaction. It is not an area permeated by the light of consciousness; consciousness can only touch it with great difficulty, yet through its workings it invades and often controls consciousness. The fable of the fisherman who acts against his best intentions according to the wishes of his (nonexistent) wife epitomizes this situation: "Frau Ilsebill, my own dear wife, wants what *I* never wanted in my life." Psychology has named this area the subconscious. This term is not altogether appropriate, first because this subconscious is present to consciousness, shows itself in and through consciousness, and attempts to have its way there. Second, if there are whole libraries of books describing "the subconscious," how can it really be "subconscious"? Third, because the whole sphere of what we called subconscious in earlier times has today become not only well known, but also actually controls a large part of our daily life. This does not mean that there is less subconscious material today than ever before, but rather that the subconscious contents undergo a shift over time. Nevertheless, we will still use the term because at that moment when the finished patterns unfold their workings in consciousness, consciousness does not want these effects and they go by largely unnoticed. Afterward consciousness can reflect on the preceding occurrence and see through it. For example, why and how I ended up in Greenland when I was concentrating on my necktie. My aunt gave me the tie as a present, and her husband gave me a book about the discovery of the North Pole when I was a child, and in this book I first read about Greenland. An emotional motivation can be found here too: I always admired my uncle for his air of being a man of the world, but to my great distress he never paid much attention to me.

In general, associations arise not according to logic but as a result of subjective experiences. They belong to the private area of the mind, even if in response to a given phrase or sight many people have the same or similar associations. Advertisement depends on this phenomenon, as does the entertainment industry. Otherwise everyone would have their own private bar or nightclub. We are not really individuals with regard to the subconscious even if we have the feeling that our emotions are completely private. To the best of my knowledge, envy, vanity, and ambition are feelings of the widest currency. I know of no one who wants to be vain, or who has set himself the goal of becoming an egotist (if he wasn't one already). "I am determined to be a villain," says Shakespeare's Richard III; but then, he already is a villain.

And yet these phenomena do have a private character, because they are not communicable. I never give up hoping that my thoughts will be understood by others, but I know that no one else can feel my feelings if I am unsuccessful in love. From descriptions they give it may appear that others have gone through similar experiences, but it is part of the nature of these feelings to be subjective. In the same way the formation of chains of associations varies subjectively, individually, even if several people have gone through similar adventures in life. A great portion of the feelings and associations themselves is also entirely subjective.

When we look at the deeper layers of the subconscious, it becomes harder and harder to describe and communicate what we find. We attempt to do it through speaking, through sentences and words by which we express our thoughts. Thoughts can be expressed more or less adroitly, pictorially, or plastically, depending on word choice and sentence structure. But we always trust that the listener will understand. Without this trust we would keep silent, and we would especially lack the courage to discuss these very themes we are now describing.

Consciously or unconsciously, we always assume that our thinking is comprehensible to all. Thus we even try to communicate our feelings through thoughts spoken aloud, whereas it would be comic to try to communicate thoughts by means of feelings. If this latter does occur, it is known as demagoguery. No thoughts are stimulated, just will impulses in the absence of all thinking. Writers of advertisements and demagogues never address the thinking human being. They attempt to bring up associations and emotions while avoiding all logical thinking as much as possible. They address that region of the soul that consists of finished contents, structures, chains of associations, rather than its unfinished, unformed capacities. Nor do they have any desire to awaken or to develop such free capacities.

It often happens that we do not understand someone's thoughts or that we believe them to be false, illogical, or not really thoughts at all. Then we have a discussion to try to explain our own point of view. How? With thoughts clothed in language. In other words, we still have complete trust in thinking: we trust that it guides us to the truth and that our partner in discussion can be brought to true insight through our thoughts. Whether or not this is successful does not for the moment concern us. One thing is important: in thinking and in the forms in which it appears, such as language, mimicry, gestures, pointing, writing (all subsumed under the word language), we discover a universal rather than private element, an element by which we communicate with others in which we can come to mutual understanding with others, or with ourselves.

We know that many thinkers doubt the communal nature of thinking or the capacity of thinking to achieve an agreement between human beings. But even this doubt depends on thinking, unless it is a mere freak of expression. We can find reasons why we should not trust thinking, but these reasons are themselves discovered through thinking. We simply cannot renounce thinking: even the decision to do so would be an act of thinking. "From now on we will obey the emotions alone": This is simply another thought. We cannot step out of our thinking unless we either give up our humanity or find something even lighter and more illuminating than thinking. For the moment, it is without doubt the clearest function of consciousness. Someone who says, "Thinking is worthless," is like a man sawing off the branch on which he is seated, because the assertion is still a thought, a thought conclusion based perhaps on unpleasant experiences.

Kant's attempt to show by his "antinomies" (mutually exclusive thought processes) that thinking is unreliable, actually proves just the opposite. Kant introduces certain arguments, for example, in favor of both the finitude and the infinitude of the universe. He wants to prove that thinking can represent both viewpoints, so that a decision between the two based on thinking is impossible. Whether or not he is right we will not debate. But if he were correct, then this story would only prove that Kant has the use of a thinking process that can discover the insufficiency of the thinking by which the two lines of argument were made. *This* thinking he characteristically "forgets," and his attempts only express his deep but not conscious trust in thinking.

Thoughts come from thinking. But where does thinking come from? What does thinking have to do with language?

These questions will lead us from the subconscious contents of the soul to the opposite pole.

Speaking and Thinking

Speaking and thinking are the public activities of consciousness by which communication among humans is possible. In earlier times they were called "spiritual" abilities. Speaking includes words revealed through writing, gestures, pointing, and mime—all the forms of intentional expression that reach others through sense perception. The human requirement for a communication involving sense perception is caused by the structure of human consciousness, which separates us from one another in consciousness. As trivial as this assertion may seem, it does not represent the only possible state of affairs. So-called primitive peoples lived and still live today in a more or less communal tribal or family consciousness. In the child's acquisition of language we always have this paradox presented to us: how can a being who neither speaks nor thinks learn words, language, and thinking? The first word, the first words, have to be understood by the child without words or explanations. Don't think that pointing, mime, and so on, would help. These signs would have to be already familiar to the child if they were to help him understand a word. If a child can understand pointing, then he long ago learned to speak, because he understands "I'm showing you this." There is no "natural" pointing gesture. The child cannot know—and *does* not know initially—that he is supposed to look in the direction of my index finger. Dogs also do not understand this gesture.

Besides, the child would have to guess what I mean to point *at:* the table, its color, the wood, the rectangle, the horizontal plane, its even proportions, all of which I can indicate with one and the same gesture. Children understand their first words directly, without words, intuitively. Or, to put it another way, they understand through such a deep internal imitation of the speaker that they "imitate" not only the words but the meaning of the intended speech. They identify themselves with the source of speaking, which is the "I" of the speaker. They have no other way of understanding anything: no explanations are possible. The meaning of the first words is understood through wordless, speechless understanding, an understanding of the speaker's thoughts or more exactly of his thought intention. Because children directly understand the thinking that the speaker seeks to express, they know what the words mean.

Many thinkers are of the opinion that children learn to speak in the same way as parrots. This is an error. Parrots cannot speak at all, any more than tape recorders can, because they do not *understand*. Children do understand; otherwise they would only repeat phrases they had already heard, and in inappropriate situations. They could not form a new sentence from familiar words to correspond to new circumstances. Yet children manage to do all this very early on.

We can observe this most clearly in the understanding of the words "I" and "you." The adult points to a table and says "Table"; the child points to the table and says "Table." The adult points to a chair and says "Chair"; the child points to the chair and says "Chair." Now the adult points to himself or herself and says "I." If the child were now to behave according to the previous pattern, he or she would point to the speaker, the adult, and say "I." Perhaps the child actually does so at first. But then he or she *understands* and says "You." Otherwise the child would logically call the speaker "I" and himself or herself "You." And this would then alternate down through the generations!

The intuitive, wordless understanding of the first words, which is actively based on the adult's comprehension of each concept, may be obscured by the use of explanations (which, in turn, must themselves be understood in order for them to explain anything). This wordless understanding is not the only accomplishment of the child's intelligent faculties. Children's ability to speak with grammatical correctness so early remains one of the great, unsolved riddles of linguistic science. Children can construct grammar (in the technical sense) at an early age, even though they have no notion of the existence of grammar and have heard only insufficient data in the form of grammatical models. They have the capacity, the *ability*, for grammar. Children really "construct" nothing at all; rather, they use grammar in practice and speak flawlessly. This applies even to syntax and sentence structure, whose rules to a great extent have not yet been formulated by linguistic science.

May I ask you a personal question? Are you familiar as an adult with the grammar of your mother tongue? And, if you have studied grammar, do you actually speak in accordance with what you have studied, or do you simply speak as you have been accustomed to do since childhood? We thus realize that speaking remains a superconscious ability throughout our lives, just as it was developed intuitively and superconsciously in childhood.

Animals communicate but do not speak. By this I mean that their communication is instinctive; they cannot consider whether or not they should give a signal. They either have to do so, or they have to *not* do so. There is no conscious intention in the process of giving or not giving signals. You may say that many people also do not always consider whether or not they should speak; they just chatter away. This all too well-known phenomenon should make us wonder about such speaking.

We can ask yet another question. The child imitates sounds and words he has heard. How does he know how to do this? What movements in the speech organs are necessary to reproduce the word or sound he had heard? This question is justified because the sound he has heard is in no way similar to the movements in the speech organs, and the relationship of such movements to the sound as it is brought forth is by no means clear even to adults. You would have to experiment briefly if I asked you how you make a *y* sound, and a really exact observation would require great effort.

Here is yet a further question in this regard, no less paradoxical: how do children learn to think? It happens with no specific instruction. To teach thinking would only be possible, and difficult even then, if children could already think. Yet after hearing and understanding the first few thoughts spoken aloud, children can form and express new thoughts on their own. They can also develop a great number of inexplicable concepts—inexplicable even to adults. Take for instance the words *yes, is, in, but,* and *love,* all words that children know how to use at a very early age. Try to explain these words to an adult. The attempt will prove deeply instructive.

For a small child, every joke is new and has to be freshly understood. This applies to every word, every concept, every thought. There are no habits of speech, no finished thought forms, no stimulus-response automatisms in the child just learning to think and to speak. These contents of adult consciousness are formed through the very faculties that the child acquires superconsciously, by means of the speech and behavior of his or her human surroundings. Without such surroundings no child will speak, or stand upright, or even be able to live, even if he or she is provided for materially.

By observing the child's acquisition of speech and thought, we can see that this process requires the faculties of thinking, feeling, and willing in order for the child to develop into a speaking adult. Yet these faculties function quite differently in the child and adult. We might say that they are not yet separated from one another for the child, but form a single faculty. The child must be able to mimic even the speech will of the speaker in order to understand, before he or she can rely on words, mime, or gesture. The meaning, the significance of the spoken word, is already contained in this speech will. Only later (perhaps not chronologically later but always *essentially* later) the meaning of the words is formed. The speech will also contains the feeling by which the spoken words are accompanied, the feeling with which one turns to talk to the child, and this feeling corresponds both to the spoken words and to the child. The feeling becomes marked both by the spoken content and also by the child to whom the content is addressed. In an optimal learning situation, the speaker's attention would be *entirely* directed toward the child. Because this ideal occurs less and less often, there are more and more children either linguistically or behaviorally handicapped.

The Superconscious

In the speech acquisition of children we have come to know a new quality of consciousness. It might be called a super-conscious ability, for the ability to speak grammatically with proper syntax, to mimic words and sounds as they are heard, and to understand wordlessly what has been said is definitely a faculty, a capacity, an *ability,* and not a *knowledge.* Words only play a role in understanding after they have already been understood themselves. Consciousness then constitutes itself as an I-consciousness out of the understood and remembered elements, and so it is actually self-evident that this conscious-ness would be ignorant of the primal understanding of the child, by which the I-consciousness came into existence. It was not present before its own birth. Later, as adults, we have little experience of this primal understanding, and so we remain unaware of our origins. When was the last time you had a new thought?

The term superconscious, therefore, is appropriate. The superconscious is always an ability, a capacity, not a habit. It is nothing finished. We found finished conscious contents in our examination of thinking, feeling, and willing. We have also seen that these finished elements in the soul are not often conscious in their effects; they are not willed by the autono-mous "I." Thus, unasked-for feelings and unintended asso-ciations arise. We can call the whole area of finished soul contents the subconscious. There is a subconscious origin to those preformed processes, such as feeling and thought forms, behavioral patterns, and will impulses, which appear without one's autonomous will in one's consciousness and sometimes overwhelm it.

The significant difference between superconscious abilities and subconscious habits consists in this very "finished" quality: the subconscious effects are always finished and come to light already formed, for example, as associations. The superconscious powers or abilities, on the other hand, because they exist at a more primal level of being are always unfinished essences, through which formed and finished products can come about. What is the difference between a habit and an ability? It would be habit if I could only play one piece on the piano, even if I could play this one piece perfectly. It would be a capacity or ability, on the other hand, if I could learn to play any given piece according to my own technical and musical ability. One can never say that a capacity is finished. There is also a difference here as to how we acquire habits and capacities. Habits are formed by regular, repeated activity or by training as one trains an animal; capacities are formed by instruction. The distinction between these two has nearly disappeared from today's schools.

The second essential distinction between these two unconscious areas consists in man's ascent, through these superconscious abilities, into a superpersonal region of being, a region that is more universal from the standpoint of thinking although it is governed by no single language. The subconscious, on the contrary, is always private in character, and has a private history. Every communication, including all art and all artisanry, is of superconscious origin.

We have seen that the forms of the subconscious, however individual in development, are nevertheless very similar to each other. We could call them collective. How then do they differ from the collectivity of the superconscious? Here is a possible analogy. Health is the natural condition of *every* organism; diseases have to attack each organism separately, but the individual cases of disease may resemble one another in their symptoms. Each of us gets sick individually, but the illness is still flu or whooping cough for everyone.

Habits, above all in childhood, are helpful and necessary, although an excess is to be avoided. When adulthood is reached, one should entirely revise one's acquired habits in order to form and practice new ones *consciously*.

Normally the level of accomplishment children attain in learning to speak and think is never attained again in the course of later life. Everything following is based on the faculties developed in childhood. We can even make the observation that, as the superconscious faculties form finished contents and habits, the faculties themselves tend to recede. A second language can then be mastered only with great difficulty, whereas children can effortlessly acquire two mother tongues if their environment is bilingual. Yet even in the adult, access to the superconscious is not altogether closed off. Every halfway normal human being can form new concepts and have new thoughts: these are intuitive flashes from the superconscious, which is always *present*, although not consciously so. This kind of presence answers many unresolved questions. The capacity of consciousness to give itself an account of its own past character can now be understood as the hidden presence of the superconscious. From this higher vantage point the gaze can look down on the phenomena and past character of consciousness. It is possible from this higher perspective to improvise real thinking, that is to say, *new* thinking, although only the already thought becomes conscious.

We can most easily see the activity of the superconscious in the life of consciousness when we examine thinking and speaking, the faculties of communication. These faculties arise in childhood and then become manifest in adulthood, although for the adult any discernment of the superconscious essence of these faculties becomes obscured through thought forms, that is, through the use of the finished products of the superconsciousness. The workings of the superconscious are actually tangible in the thought process. In addition, we can at least get an inkling of superconscious *feeling* by noticing our ability to decide whether a given sentence makes sense or contains mere gibberish—either of which is possible, even if the sentence is grammatically and linguistically correct. Authors, lecturers, journalists, politicians, and scientists have developed such virtuosity with language that it is often difficult to notice the emptiness of what they are saying. If you ask yourself how you know that something is logical or illogical and why, then you will find that you do not really make a comparison with the formalities of logical theory. Such comparisons would also require the faculty you do in fact use, which is a feeling, a *cognizing feeling* of logicality, in accord with which your thinking proceeds if it is real thinking. Your thinking follows this feeling superconsciously. Logic is not a prescriptive science ("You must think this way") but an afterthought, a subsequent description of how thinking actually proceeds. If people did not already think logically without studying logic, they would never be prompted to study it, to say nothing of the authors of books on logic, who would never have been able to write them if they had not previously read what they were about to write! No author can quote his works before he has written them. Insofar as the human being thinks, he thinks logically. If a logical error is committed, then the blame belongs not to thinking, but to the not-thinking that has found its way into the stream of thought, otherwise we could never discover the failure of thought by thinking about it. What guides our thinking in its logical course is a distinct *feeling of clarity*, the feeling that something is being made evident.

We can also have some idea of a quite distinct will, all too clear and distinct, in fact, for our normal consciousness. The "dark" will takes hold of our bodily actions, and it cannot be consciously followed. But when we think very concentratedly, improvisationally, how do we do it? We consciously determine what we will think about, then we let thinking itself take over, while we calm our subjective willfulness as much as possible. There is a particular kind of will hidden within this will that we have allowed to take control. *I* do not think a particular thing; I don't even know what thought will come up in the next moment. The will in this improvisational thinking is at one with the thinking itself. It is a thought will and is not willed by *me*. In pure, concentrated thinking, there is always this superconscious will. In this will, in turn, the feeling for what is evident (which propels thinking) also lies hidden. Can I say that this will is my own? Not at all; I merely set it in motion, and I am not even conscious of how I do so.

The process of perceiving is very similar. Here the attention alone is willfully brought about by us; *what* is perceived is utterly beyond our will. We cannot willingly change anything about it: we cannot see green as yellow. The will of the perceptual world itself determines what we see. It depends on us, on our conceptual world, on our attention, and so on. These determine how deeply we can see and live into whatever presents itself. As we let the perceptual world "speak" to us more, and we allow ourselves to interrupt it less, we will find our perceptions become more complete. We must allow this alien will meeting us to hold sway. It is a reverse kind of will, because it does not go from us toward the world, but flows from the world toward us. This reverse will also comes from the superconscious.

Man and His World

The human being breathes back and forth between the realm of the already formed and the realm of pure abilities. We could also say that he is breathed by them. The already formed elements in the soul combine themselves with the part of the human being that is naturally preformed: his corporeality. Universal abilities, the possibilities of creating forms, come from the other side; they are spiritual abilities. They come from a world, the world of the spirit, which cannot at first be consciously experienced by man. This world is common to all human beings, and reveals itself in the conscious world by the fact that humans can intentionally communicate with one another. It is also shown in the two universal elements of the conscious world, thinking and perceiving, the elements that constitute the conscious world of mankind. They make this world what it is according to the thinking and perceiving of a given historical epoch. As forces,

33

as abilities, as formative elements, they obviously cannot derive from the world that they themselves build, which they themselves have formed. They come from a hidden world of the spirit, and emerge into the human experience of consciousness as superconscious soul elements. We know them as our own abilities to think, perceive, and form mental pictures. The spiritual world from which they come clearly borders closely on the world of consciousness.

What we call everyday normal consciousness is not yet present in the child just learning to speak and think. This consciousness is formed through speaking and thinking, which in this phase constitute a *single* process. The subconscious, finished, associatively bound thought forms, feeling patterns, habits of feeling, and habits of willing are all absent from the young child. The child presents a clean slate, to a large extent, so as to be able to learn any language spoken in his environment, independently of his heredity. We see the child's individuality in the superconscious selection of only certain impressions from among many. The child ignores a great deal that to all appearances ought to make an impression.

What we call fate makes itself evident partly in the instinctive acceptance of certain impulses and the rejection of others. We can observe great variations in behavior within a single family, and there are similar variations in character and in the relationship with the surrounding world. Such variations occur even between twins. The selective forces are superconscious, as are specific gifts such as an aptitude for music or mathematics, for example, which may emerge very early on. The subconscious and the habits of consciousness are built up later under the influence of the environment, yet even these follow a superconscious selectivity pattern, in which we recognize the individual's predisposition to a particular fate. We could say that the superconscious, including the pattern of selectivity, is the origin, and normal consciousness builds itself up through the activity of superconscious abilities. The subconscious, meanwhile, represents what we might call the negative of individuality—it reveals what the

34

individuality scorned and therefore distorted.

Subconscious impulses rise up "from below" into adult consciousness while new concepts and intuitions shine in "from above." The adult's conscious life is a stage in which what is most private and what is most universal appear simultaneously. Even thinking and perceiving consist of these two elements. In thinking the human being's activity is to choose the theme or subject matter, and this activity stands in the foreground, whereas the "how" of thinking, its logicality and evidentness, originate in the superconscious and are therefore noticeable in consciousness only as borderline states. In perceiving, the human contribution is more hidden; it comprises the necessary attention, the concepts, and the capacity to form concepts that determine our perceptual picture. It can be very instructive for an understanding of one's own consciousness to look for the part of thinking that does not stem from everyday consciousness, and on the other hand to seek for that aspect of perception that is the result of human participation.

You may well think, this author does not even address the most widely held scientific views, according to which thinking, perceiving, mental pictures, and the whole life of consciousness are derived from the activity of the brain and nervous system. There are even various different models of this activity, and so the superconscious or the spiritual world are superfluous and false as explanatory principles or hypotheses. I would like to demonstrate in the next chapter that such views are signs of a fundamental disease in consciousness.

2

THE DISEASED
CONSCIOUSNESS

The Soul's Problems

The soul's present awareness has separated from its past elements, and can now observe them from the outside. This state of affairs makes our entire discussion possible. When we say separated or disentangled, we presuppose a previous state of entanglement, when the two were blended together. In fact, there was a phase of human development during which discussions of consciousness, logic, thinking, and so on, were intelligible to only a very few. Most people could not understand these words and concepts, just as today a child younger than about seven years old cannot grasp concepts having to do with the life of consciousness. The child understands the word *speaking* but not the word *language*, because his thinking has not yet separated itself from his speaking; he actually thinks in the words of his mother tongue. This kind of consciousness is much livelier than what comes later, but the liveliness is lived through as in a dream. Consciousness dwells within what is experienced, rather than outside it or opposed to it. As adults we encounter unexpected events in this same fashion, that is to say, not in full presence of mind judging the event from outside, but with a muffled, dreamlike awareness.

Today every more or less normal adult has some grasp of words and concepts that relate to consciousness. A second process parallels this separation of present and past elements in consciousness: the number and the intensity of mental problems increases continually, both for the individual and for mankind as a whole. Even in children we see that a small child normally has fewer mental problems than a slightly older child, apart from the ever-increasing number of cases in which an unhealthy adult environment affects the child prematurely. Today a far greater percentage of normal people are nervous or unstable than a hundred years ago—and two hundred years ago even fewer were in need of psychological or psychiatric care. The patients in question are predominantly the city dwellers and the well educated. It is hard to understand our own findings here. The newfound possibility of observing consciousness should not have led to more problems: we would have expected, on the contrary, that this possibility would allow mental difficulties to be handled and cured consciously. Perhaps these mental problems arise from the failure to actually realize the new possibilities of the soul. Unused capacities or positive possibilities transform themselves into something harmful, into diseases or negative symptoms: this amounts to a law of nature as well as a law of consciousness. The teeth of certain rodents, if unused, can cause the rodent's own death.

From this viewpoint, we will now attempt to examine the symptoms of the disease of consciousness. We are led to this by our conviction that behind the multiplicity of individual mental difficulties, there lurks a single collective disease of consciousness that goes unnoticed *because* it is collective: who could notice it? In fantasy accounts describing "the country of the blind," blindness is not reckoned a handicap; in fact, it goes unrecognized. If a foreigner who can see strays into such a country, he would do well not to mention his "abnormal" ability, otherwise the well-meaning natives may

37

"cure" him of his "hallucinations."

The reader might be wondering, if the disease is collective, how I became aware of it. The answer to this question will be given at the end of the book.

The Denial of Cognition

Through the separation of the present from the past elements in consciousness, the present element rises into the super-conscious and it is no longer experienced directly. Meanwhile, the thoughts, perceptions, and mental pictures that remain behind in the field of consciousness—as "seen" from the superconscious, which does not experience itself—become clearer and sharper. In other words, while the *production* of consciousness is not conscious, not experienced, the *product* becomes all the more distinct. The finished, lifeless picture is clearly outlined because it is no longer animated by anything living.

Before the disengagement of the producing element from its product, there was more fantasy at work in consciousness. Remember the late medieval heroic sagas and legends (already an object of ridicule for Cervantes). There were giants, dragons, fantastic animals, magicians, sprites, and other fairy-tale beings, all cheerfully combined with descriptions of travel, foreign peoples, and countries. None of this remains in the age of the consciousness-soul, as we will call the present compartmentalized structure of the psyche. On the other hand, the possibility arises of reflecting both upon cognition and understanding, and upon the creative activity and ability of man that enables us to know about consciousness. This activity is not itself directly experienced, but since the "already cognized" continually changes, and grows in quantity, it seems natural to conclude that there is a source, a process from which and by which the clearly experienced contents of consciousness arise. People cut off from sense perceptions will notice that their thinking comes from a source, a process within them. Human beings could, then, in principle, address themselves to this process of cognition. That would be thoroughly logical given the constellation of their consciousness. Yet the "sight" of this cognition, of their activity in knowing, in its active, producing essence, is ignored. Cognition is denied and cut off from any claim to reality—a denial that can take many forms, although they all are symptoms of the same disease. We always use cognition, even at the moment that we disavow it. Is there anything that is neither the result of cognition nor the content of cognition? Directly or indirectly —as in an obvious lie—cognition is always at work.

The exclusion of cognition from reality has three mutually connected forms, one of which is the real source of the error. This first fundamental form of the disease was touched on in Section 1.2. It is the doubt of thinking, a doubt that is itself thought up and formulated by means of thinking. This is well illustrated by the following letter.

Prof. Zeno Bubbleblower
Dept. of Logic

Dear Colleague,

Allow me to make the following observations with regard to your last lecture at the philosophical society in Sprawlsville. First, there is no such thing as thinking; it is only a disease of the brain. Man is a machine, and therefore does not exist. In brief, I do not exist and you do not exist. Why do you bother to give lectures? It is quite illogical. All discourse is untenable; all speech is superfluous.

With collegial respect,

Henry Overproof
PROF. OF CRITICAL PHILOSOPHY

You might suppose that this kind of thing could be written only by some insane philosopher. But no, we all maintain the same level of discourse whenever we regard ourselves as determined beings, as natural phenomena, as the results of heredity, environment, circumstances, or fate—or when we see ourselves as a mass of cells or a heap of molecules. Whenever, in fact, we do not wish to take responsibility for ourselves.

The correspondence between our professors could continue. After receiving the first letter, Prof. Bubbleblower would reply: You are right. But then your own letter is nothing other than. . . . Prof. Overproof would write back: Naturally, but your own letter therefore is nothing other than . . . . You can imagine for yourself the continuation of this exchange.

The whole issue becomes very simple when put so crudely. It goes like this: "I am not," "I do not exist," "I am not here." *Can* anyone say this? Obviously not. The sentences are all grammatically correct, and contain no contradiction within themselves. The contradiction comes when we grasp not only the contents of the utterance, but the uttering and the utterer. If someone speaks, and maintains at the same time that he does not exist, or is not present in the place where he is speaking, then there is a contradiction. The same holds true for "You are not" or "You are not here." At best, that could be said in a monologue if I were looking for someone I could not find and then commented on this result out loud. But the sentence cannot be taken seriously if I direct it to a you—who is not there.

There is an ancient logical riddle, the Cretan paradox: "All Cretans are liars," says a Cretan, or more simply, "I am lying." These are impossible utterances. If all Cretans are liars and always lie, then the utterance of this Cretan is also a lie: but if it is a lie, then the sentence could also be true, namely if just now the speaker has not lied. But then the utterance really is a lie, because here is at least one exception to the allegedly continual lying of the Cretans, and so on. Why is it possible to say "All Cretans always tell the truth" or "I am telling the truth"? Because here, in contrast to the lying sentences, the *content* of the utterance does not contradict the fact of its being uttered. Any logic that does not take the utterance itself into consideration will never escape from the paradox of the Cretan liar.

What does all this mean? It points out the necessity of taking into account not only the content, but *the fact of utterance*. If we do this, then a whole list of utterances becomes impossible. They cancel themselves out, as with the utterance of the Cretan liar. An example of such an utterance is the sentence "The brain thinks." This simple formula encapsulates all the views that trace thinking to natural processes. Because such processes occur in the brain and nervous system, thinking is supposed to have its source and origin there, and to be causally dependent on such processes. We shall first take up this assertion purely as a matter of thought; then we shall consider the role of the brain in thinking.

That various processes occur in the brain during thinking is a well-researched reality. It is well known that wounds to the brain hinder thinking or certain thought patterns. Yet these facts do not in any way require us to think of the brain as the cause of thinking. As a model for this, we can imagine a violinist and his violin. Without an instrument, the greatest virtuoso cannot play music. If the violin is only slightly damaged, the music is immediately and seriously affected. But to conclude from this that the music is made by the violin would be nonsense. In fact, no one thinks so.

From all observed phenomena there is no reason to represent the role of the brain by a model that would correspond to the judgment that "the brain thinks." But if we were to suppose for a moment that thinking really does proceed from the brain, then it would have to come about through natural processes. Natural processes are either determined or accidental. This means that in principle or in practice we cannot follow the causal links between them. If thinking comes about as a result of a predetermined natural process, then thinking is also predetermined. In this case it is meaningless to speak of error or truth in regard to thinking or knowing (and the way we know things today is shot through with thinking). Predetermined natural processes cannot go wrong —the term would be meaningless applied to them. We can only talk about errors when we have discovered them as

41

such. We never intentionally produce errors: we try to arrive at truth and only later does it turn out, occasionally, that we have made an error. This would mean that after a predetermined natural process had made an "error" (already meaningless), the same natural process discovers and corrects the error. There are no such natural processes. Imagine a mathematician who checks the validity of one kind of thinking by means of that very same thinking, without relying on any outside element.

If brain activity proceeds by accidents, that is, if what we call thought is an accidental effect, then the possibility of error does arise, but we have the task of distinguishing between the good accidental results ("correct" thoughts) and nonthoughts. By means of *what*? We have no tool to use but thinking—the same accidental procedure that gave us what we are trying to check. Experience shows us, however, that we *generally* can distinguish between thought and nonthought, and the distinction is made not by using a measurement outside the realm of thought, but through thought alone, through our feeling for what is evident, the feeling of "that's obvious; that's clear to me."

Not only do we notice and correct failures of thought: it is worth realizing that in a discussion of the predetermination or dependence of the thought process, these qualities have to be *noticed*. But how and by whom? If *everything* is predetermined, including all the processes in the system, if consciousness is causally dependent on its physical apparatus, then there would be no authority, no tribunal, to perceive this dependence, this predetermination. A causally determined system can *notice* neither its own predetermined character nor anything else: its functions are all determined; it merely *reacts* to causal factors. The causal factors in question, for thinking as for perceiving, are identical with the physiological processes in the brain. Yet we must assume that consciousness is something other than the physical and chemical processes in the brain even if it is wholly dependent on them, or exists in response to them. Consciousness knows nothing in the beginning of the brain's functions: it must investigate the brain from outside, anatomically, or by means of machines like the encephalograph. By itself, thinking does not reveal any connection with the head, just as seeing does not immediately point to its own physical apparatus. And so, because the thinker knows nothing of all this, the dependence of thinking has to be ascertained from the outside by an observer who not only notices what thought process is accompanied by what brain activity, but who also determines that the thought process is *caused* by the brain (a concertgoer, following this method, would conclude that the bow moves the violinist's right arm).

Everyone knows how the whole world seems to change depending on whether one feels healthy or has a stomachache. This experience seems to be a proof that consciousness depends upon our physical condition. If this dependence were *total,* that is, if consciousness were entirely the result of the state of the stomach, then it would be impossible to notice this state of dependence. The discovery is made only because consciousness is not *entirely* dependent. It surveys both health and disease, and, through a comparison of the two, perceives a state of dependence. This state is not absolute, because the one-who-perceives, the act of noticing, has not itself been accounted for. Here we discover once again the fundamental symptom of the diseased consciousness.

Natural processes, nerve processes, physical and chemical processes—we can know and speak about such things because a consciousness cognizes them. Natural processes cannot *cognize* themselves; they can only affect each other and react to one another. They can influence one another, reproduce one another indirectly or transformatively, yet all this is not cognition, it is not seeing or thinking, but merely the external side of the process of consciousness. They are side phenomena, or physical processes necessary for consciousness in the same way that processes taking place in the violin are necessary for music to be heard. But even the most complex physical process can never imitate or reproduce the internal aspect of consciousness, the experience of consciousness, let alone *become* the experience. The physical process remains a physical process, it remains outside as seen from the life of consciousness. An example will make this clearer.

If you want to know what time it is, you look at your watch. The watch "tells" the time. Does the watch know what time it is? No one would claim it does, because the watch has no consciousness. Now, let's take a so-called repeating watch. When you press a button it tolls out the time down to the last quarter hour. It can be asked and it can answer. Does this clock know what time it is? Clockmakers, at least, will not agree to this, nor would anyone who is not utterly naive. Now we take a giant step forward: we construct a watch so that when I ask it "Dear Elisa, what time is it?" the watch answers in English, telling me the time to the nearest second. And even more, it recognizes my voice. If *you* were to ask it the time, it would say, "I'll have nothing to do with you. You are not my master." And even if I am the one to ask, but I do not put it politely enough, the watch will answer only, "That's no way to talk to me."

Does *this* watch know what time it is? Perhaps you are already uncertain. Consider that this watch is only a more complicated mechanism than the ordinary wristwatch. It experiences nothing, has no consciousness, and does not know what time it is, even if it can "say" the time. Does such a watch really *speak?* We leave this question open, for the moment. The clock imitates the abilities of a human consciousness *from the outside.* For this, a human consciousness had to construct and program it, regulating the mechanism to work in the desired fashion. And if it was constructed automatically, then a human consciousness had to be there to plan, construct, and program the mechanism that made the clock. Even though a mechanism, an apparatus, is necessary for consciousness, consciousness cannot be created by a machine, no matter how complex.

We should be done with the superstition that a physical process can cause something other than a physical process; and we should also be done with the superstition that if the machine is sufficiently complex a consciousness will arise within it of its own accord. We have seen by the example of the distracted, daydreaming child that something else is necessary for us to become conscious. When either a child or an adult has a finger near a candle flame, the finger will be drawn away. This is a process guided by a sentient consciousness. We can easily produce the same process mechanically by using a simple heat-sensitive metallic device whose shape changes according to temperature. Today, such heat-sensitive elements can be found as safety devices in many gas appliances. If they "feel" no warmth, the pilot light is out and they shut off the gas supply. Does the appliance *feel* warmth? Does it know whether it is warm or not?

A physical process occurs in the appliance, but it has no consciousness of this process. In the brain, a physical process also occurs: this process alone is analogous to what takes place in the appliance, and, as in the gas safety device, this process is not consciousness. Someone who considers the soul, the consciousness, as a similar but more complicated mechanism, may not see the distinction here. For such a person, every mousetrap is "alive": it "notices" the mouse and bites it.

A further question would be: which one is primary, the physical process or the process of consciousness? Doctor Skullskins would like to prove that my brain is responsible for my thoughts. He attaches electrodes from an encephalograph to my head and proposes to show me the different signals and graph curves that the machine writes out according to whether I am thinking, fantasizing, or dreaming. I sit down in a chair, and everything is prepared. Then Doctor Skullskins turns to me and says, "Now, Mr. Kühlewind, please think the following thought: 'Two plus two equals four.' " Did you hear that? He asks *me*; *I* am supposed to think about two plus two. And he asks so politely! But if my brain were the *cause* of all thought, why should he address *me*, what do *I* have to do with it all? He should deal with my brain, if that is the cause. Or does he intend *me* to pass on his request to my brain? It seems that this is what he has in mind, in which case I am, after all, an important part of the process. I can fool him at this point: instead of thinking

"Two plus two equals four," I can call to mind a cops-and-robbers film or the opera *Boris Godunow*. Or instead of "two plus two," I can think simply "Now I'll fool you." Or I can silently recite something from A.A. Milne. But I can also comply with the doctor's request. After all, it was so polite—it all depends on me. What I am to think depends entirely on me and furthermore, what my brain does depends on me. When I choose something, waves appear on the screen of the measuring apparatus according to what *I* have decided. In any event, *I* have to begin and then the brain follows, moment by moment. Halfway through my "two plus two" I can decide to recite Bilbo Baggins' traveling song from the *Lord of the Rings:* I desire it and my brain follows suit, more or less like the bow and violin played by Mr. Szering. Is there no case in which the brain is the determinative partner? Certainly—at least when I have a headache. Also when I fall into a chain of associations (see Foreword once again). But when I am wide awake, then the brain obeys me quite completely. And because I can decide each moment how I will behave in the next moment—especially when this question of the encephalograph gets me excited—there are no grounds for claiming that my brain is responsible for my thinking. I bear the responsibility for *who I am,* as we have just proved experimentally. And by addressing me, as he must to begin the experiment, the doctor shows that he is also of this opinion. Only he doesn't know it yet. Without his asking me, no previously decided upon result would come about, and so it is up to me *what* result does come about. And, what is more, no one besides myself can know what I am thinking. No one can force me to think about a particular thing. Many inquisitors, dictators, and their henchmen have already tried to find a method for forcing people to think a given thought, or to say what they are thinking. But force can, at most, make people say what their interrogators would like to hear.

If we could talk to the brain directly and if it functioned as a consciousness, then consciousness would be superfluous.

The only question would be, who is interested in talking to a brain? Would the mechanical apparatuses have a conversation? And why would they? If thinking, perceiving, and cognizing are strictly predetermined processes, then we might as well stop talking about them. No one can expect to influence a natural process by means of discussion; no one can hope to convince a plum tree to bear figs next year. Such a discussion would be even more unlikely between two plum trees.

The fact that thinking and cognizing are to some extent dependent on the body can only be ascertained by a cognizing power that is not itself dependent, and that can therefore observe this dependence as if from outside. In the same way, man would never speak and think about being determined if he were really totally determined: in that case he would never notice it and never form the concept of determination. He forms this concept and speaks about the problem only because he also knows the concept of freedom. He can know both concepts only because he is part free and part unfree. A completely free or a completely unfree being would never come across this problem. Anyone really dependent on a person or on a passion generally claims to be operating with complete freedom.

Another form of forgetting that we claim or utter something, is to hold the opinion that there exists a reality altogether independent of cognition: that human consciousness or cognition merely makes images of this reality, more or less faithfully, as in a not quite perfect mirror. Apart from its validity, we can ask the question: who holds such an opinion? Someone who knows of reality only through this "mirroring," this "imaging," knows only images or reflections. How does he know that they are images? To claim what he knows is the reflection or image of reality that exists independently of imaging and reflecting, he would have to be able to perceive this reality from the outside, without reflection or imaging, as well as the mirror itself and the process of mirroring, that is, he would have to somehow be in contact with reality directly. This might be God almighty, but certainly

47

not man: man has knowledge only through his consciousness, and if this consciousness is a reflecting or imaging machine, then man knows only reflected images. He can say nothing of any reality outside these images. Besides consciousness there is no other access, no hotline to reality.

It is the same with the claim that truth is the correspondence of representation or of theory (thinking) with reality. In order to ascertain or test such a correspondence, one would have to already know reality so as to compare it with the theory. But if we know reality, why do we need further questions? Why would we need representations and theories and what would we compare to what in order to find correspondences? We behave at times as if reality were a sausage and theory something like an estimate of the length of the sausage, and our only job is to compare the sausage's length with our estimate.

Man's greatest problem is not knowing what reality is. If we knew that, we would have nothing more to ask.

A vase with flowers in it stands on the table; I see it. If asked why I see it, I answer candidly, "Because it's there." And how do I know it's there? "Because I see it." All this doesn't sound too logical. And there is something not quite right about our logic anyway. In school we were taught that man drew logical conclusions through syllogisms and used them to form new pronouncements. The following example concerns Peter.

> 1. Peter is human
> 2. Humans are mortal
>
> Therefore 3. Peter is mortal

1. and 2. are called premises, conditions, or available knowledge, while 3. is called the conclusion. The syllogism is set up so that we seem to draw the conclusion statement 3. from the preceding premises—as if we didn't have to know the conclusion long beforehand in order to find the right premises. Otherwise how could we choose from the countless possible utterances or statements? Even if we decided to use the

terms "Peter" and "humans" (which is unjustified if we are really ignorant of statement 3.) we might, choosing randomly, get the following:

          1. Peter has two ears
          2. Humans are clever
Therefore 3. ???????????????????

We could look around for a long, long time before finding two sentences that go together. And then?

          1. Peter is human
          2. Humans have two ears
Therefore 3. Peter has two ears

This is just as valid and meaningful as the first conclusion that Peter is mortal. One thing is certain: no one draws conclusions in this manner. First one has the conclusion, then one can choose corresponding premises. Why are we concerned with this? Because this example can also show us how readily we forget what we are actually doing.

We said that the exclusion of cognition from the world has three forms. The first form is to forget or not to notice or take into account what we are doing at the very moment of making a statement. Our attention is concerned only with the content of the statement and doesn't focus on the act of stating itself. This not noticing leads to the second form of exclusion. Cognition, the autonomous essence that calls forth all our knowledge, is denied and attributed to the "things" it knows. Thinking is attributed to the brain, to a computerlike model, to natural processes, and so on. We can give a name to this procedure: cognition is *reduced,* traced back, to something that is not cognition or even to "noncognition"—something that itself had to be cognized by cognition! It is by no means an easy matter to hit on the notion that cognitive processes are to be traced back to the brain. That notion had to be cognized by cognition, which thereby reduces itself to brain processes. Quite apart from the question of truth or error here, which we have already dealt with, this is a fine example of Baron Münchhausen's tactics!

If the attribution of cognition to a natural process corresponded to reality, then there would be *no one* left to judge the correctness of this theory. It would be subject neither to disproof nor to confirmation. It would therefore not be a theory at all.

When we deny cognition as an autonomous truth we also deny the subject, the *I*, as a being: we become complicated automatons, and these automatons are then supposed to assert that they *are* automatons. But if they were exclusively automations, there is no way that they could have acquired such ideas. The idea of a nonautomaton must have arisen somehow. A rule is only known and formulated on the basis of at least one exception—so says B.L. Whorf, an ingenious linguist (*Language, Thought, and Reality*):

> For instance, if a race of people had the physiological defect of being able to see only the color blue, they would hardly be able to formulate the rule that they saw only blue. The term blue would convey no meaning to them, their language would lack color terms, and their words denoting their various sensations of blue would answer to, and translate, our words "light, dark, white, black," and so on, not our word "blue." In order to formulate the rule or norm of seeing only blue, they would need exceptional moments in which they saw other colors.

Because we do not consciously experience the processes of consciousness (thinking, perceiving, making mental pictures), because they remain superconscious, the *results* of these processes appear much more real than the processes themselves. Therefore we tend to derive the processes from their results, attributing the former to the latter. If, for example, thinking (which brings about the already thought) were to become as conscious as the already thought, then we would not hold thinking to be any less real than the already thought, and it would not occur to us to see in the brain or the nerves a more secure reality than in the cognition that discovers brain and nerves and ascribes to them this more secure reality. This same tendency makes us assign to cognition a merely reflective or image-making role. Reality is finished and complete without cognition. How do I know this? By cognition! As if from the outside, cognition looks in through a window into the room where reality is. Cognition, therefore, remains outside. We could then put the question, where is cognition, if not within reality?

The Causes of the Disease

Readers may ask at this point, "How can people, how can thinkers and philosophers, think so much nonsense?" The answer is that we are dealing with a collective "disease." Even the so-called mentally ill can be very clever and mentally alert and logical at times. The disease has historical causes, but we will not concern ourselves with them here. It can also be explained psychologically, as we shall attempt to show in the following chapter. At first glance there is a simple explanation: When we deny the *I*, the subject (by means of the *I*, by means of the subject, of course), then we escape from all responsibility. A very tempting situation. Then things happen to us and we have no freedom, no possibility of making new beginnings, particularly because we are not *we*, not beings. That would be a rational explanation for the phenomenon. And, like most rational thoughts, it is insufficient. In all "reductive" explanations ("Thinking is nothing other than . . . ") we notice a certain desire, a kind of lust, whose roots lie not in rationality but in feeling. There must be a cause in the soul itself to bring about so much illogicality.

Also, the authority within us (thinking cognition) that should normally detect disease is itself diseased. All diseases of consciousness are self-sealing. The more nonsense we think—or *imagine* that we are *thinking*—the more our con-

51

sciousness becomes diseased and the unnoticed, unthinking, supposedly thought through blockages in consciousness hinder thinking by their very impenetrability, something like blockages in the body's circulatory system. Mental pictures, opinions, judgments that are not clearly thought through, which have not been formed completely consciously, worsen the disease.

We have described a specialized failure of thought and pursued its consequences, insofar as these show up in thinking. A reasonable question would be, "Are these the only consequences?" We are, after all, familiar with other mental disturbances that seem to have nothing to do with what has been described.

The disease of thinking deprives the soul of the possibility of correctly assessing its own situation, because thinking is the "eye of the soul" for modern man, that is, the clearest function of his consciousness. As we have seen, it is through thinking that we orient ourselves with regard to other functions of consciousness. When thinking becomes diseased, contemporary man loses his orientation. This means that he is moved and influenced by unclear, uncontrolled, impenetrable impulses. The source of these impulses will be encountered in the next chapter. This is why the disease of thinking is so serious: in the symptoms we have described it is possible to find a great number of motifs of the worldview of today. But that is only one possible viewpoint. A general rule for the life of the soul states that any unused human capabilities transform themselves into symptoms of disease; they become sicknesses, negative forces. The next chapter will deal with this phenomenon in greater depth. Here we will consider another central cluster of questions as an example of the developmental problems brought about through the disease of consciousness.

In earlier times man was conscious of himself as a created creature and knew, not by his thinking but by an inborn natural wisdom with a correspondingly dreamlike consciousness, that he is a spiritual, ensouled being. Today in the age of the diseased consciousness, now that the existence of the I-being is denied and attributed to externally observable natural processes, man is unsure of his own feeling of existence: "Man is nothing other than . . . " The more honest a man is in his thinking, the more his own being seems to slip away from him, since his thinking tells him something quite different from what he would otherwise feel about himself. Because he does not experience thinking in "present" process, he also has no present experience of the *Thinker* and looks for his own being where only clear, contoured contents of consciousness are to be found: in the soul's *past,* in the already thought, already perceived, already mentally pictured, in the mirrored past consciousness. But the image of one's own being as something already past is just as unreal as any other image in this consciousness. And so we have to continually convince ourselves anew of our own existence; we have to find confirmation in order to feel that we *are.* We are similar to the Zen student who asks his master about the Buddha nature (we would ask about our true I-being) and receives the reply, "You're looking for the ox you're riding on."

We have arrived at the roots of egoity. Because man does not experience the Seeker, the Thinker, the Experiencer in his presentness, he needs property, success, self-assertion—confirmation that he *is.* Instead of experiencing himself as a *thinker,* which is certainly possible, he seeks to convince himself of his existence from the outside, and that brings him to the habit of self-feeling. But man can only feel himself because of *something*—everything that serves him in this way, everything important and "necessary," everything he clings to. Finally other men begin to serve the same purpose for him, and this determines his relationship to them. Position, power, money, and recognition form his world, on which he is dependent, and in which he has continually to make an effort to prove himself, to be certain of his own existence.

The disease of the soul begins, then, from above, with the soul's most luminous ability. A large part of the scientific pronouncements of today are already conditioned by the disease of consciousness: man as computer, as a physical descendant of animals, language as a result of programming, and so on. No one has yet observed a higher development or a "positive" mutation, much less a whole suite of connected mutations with a positive result. In order for man to do anything with his hands, which are neither claws nor hooves, his brain must have developed simultaneously in just the right way or both brain and hand would be only handicaps in the struggle for existence. To consider language as a result of programming, another language has to be assumed through which the programming can occur.

These ideas are myths, but dangerous myths, with a tendency to make themselves come true. "The brain thinks" is realized whenever a human starts associating instead of thinking and even considers association to *be* thinking. A disorientation occurs through the lack of self-experience in the processes of consciousness, and because of this man relies on self-feeling more than necessary, and self-feeling becomes an addiction. He cultivates a feeling life that can be called diseased because it is guided by egoity. Normal feeling feels nothing at all; it is not like an eye, but like a diseased eye which, instead of looking out, feels *itself*, itches, aches, hurts. Could this be diseased feeling? It feels only itself. And then, due to an uncertain experience of the *I*, the life of the will gets weaker and weaker. *Who* would be doing the *willing*? Especially if you are convinced that everything is determined —what would "will" mean in that case?

Science operates altogether passively with respect to the movements of the soul. We knew long ago that man is an egotistical being, but we used to be ashamed of it; it was seen as a sickness, a moral defect, generally attributed to the Fall. Today we are proud of our egotism, and somewhere I heard the phrase "sacro egoismo." It is a scientific conviction that man is originally and "naturally" an egotist, and all moral behavior is a successful taming of his fundamentally asocial, "evil" nature. But this would be to confuse a correct diagnosis of disease with the norm for health. If the whole world is a hospital for influenza sufferers, and even the doctors have the disease, then society will consider ill, and try to cure, everyone who has no cough, no fever, no congestion. Marx said, correctly, that the history and politics of his time were led primarily by the economic interests of states and social classes, a correct diagnosis of disease. As a doctor he would have said, this is the way it is, but it mustn't go on this way. But he accepted the disease, because he was also infected (only he wanted the disease to serve a different social class).

Science justifies anything. If for some reason it became fashionable to walk on all fours, physics, statistics, and orthopedics would greet it as a great step forward: a much more stable method than that balancing act on our two relatively long, thin legs. Doctors would also find advantages to it, for example, the beneficial effects on the digestive system and on blood flow to the head. Psychologists, crying "back to nature!" would discover fantastic benefits for social life: differences in height would become less noticeable, thereby leading to fewer inferiority complexes among short people with all the attendant problems of overcompensation. Economic experts would find a host of favorable effects: to clothe the hands a new kind of shoe would have to be produced and marketed, new styles, furniture, and so on, stimulating new economic growth! New films, new plays, bars, nightclubs!

Everyone needs success—and no frustrations, please! Do you really think it was always this way? That people simply fell apart when they weren't successful in something? Dante, despite his fervent desire, couldn't succeed in a political career. But we have the *Divine Comedy* as a result, which certainly would not have been written if Dante had become mayor of Florence. Certainly the diagnosis is correct that we have to be successful. But if psychology regarded this not as normality, but as a disease, then we might be cured of this state and stop the struggle for success. For this to work, however, we would have to no longer see this struggle as normal.

When the diagnosis of disease becomes the norm of health, it determines upbringing, social contact, human relations, and human behavior. If egoity is part of normal human nature, then we have to raise young egotists, which we are in fact doing with great industry, and if someone doesn't have sufficient bent in that direction, he will have to be "cured." The origin of the disease does not lie in the private, personal sphere, but in thinking, in the common communicative essence of man. From this we develop the more personal symptoms of a disturbed soul life. When nonsense "thinks," it creates more nonsense. The disease of disdaining to take up our initially superconscious capabilities creates a collective (and therefore unnoticed) subconscious. This collective subconscious becomes a world power by means of collective, infectious "inspirations" and today it rules the surface level of earthly events.

Thanks to the recent separation of present consciousness from its past elements, it would be possible for us to observe cognition and understanding as present processes and gradually to incorporate them into our experience. Instead, cognition is excluded from our worldview because we regard only the outside of consciousness, its products, its behavior. Such a mental attitude is unhealthy because

1. it disturbs the logicality, the transparency of thinking and tends toward self-annihilating statements, e.g., "I am not."

2. it makes possible a view of the world from which man is excluded. He is therefore made uncertain of his consciousness of existence—egoity, self-assertion, "self-realization."

3. it turns unrealized abilities into unhealthy, irrational instincts which, justified by science, are then "rationally" satisfied and so achieve a determinative power in our lives.

We ascribe no reality to cognition, or at most a secondary reality, while we consider the *products* of this unreal cognition to be reality. The separation of the two elements in consciousness presents a possibility which today has been only half realized: man looks at the past elements without discovering that he is looking, from his presentness, and that *he* is looking. The consequences show up in a distortion of the whole life of the soul—of the whole of life.

3

A LITTLE
PSYCHOLOGY

The Inside of the Soul

If the clearest function in the soul and spirit, by which men should be able to orient themselves, has become sick, then it is no wonder that the disease and its symptoms even appear in the guise of scientific theories. We live today in the age of the consciousness-soul, with a clear claim to conscious, scientific formulation of the nature of humanity, society, and world. It is amazing, however, that despite the intensity of the research supported by immense financial funds and a highly methodical application, despite the well-recognized central importance of science, whose influence and power have never been so great, nature, man, and society are caught today in a decline on a scale never before dreamed of. We could hardly understand all this if it were not for the insight that the life and the heart of this powerful, popular science —thinking—is diseased. We see it most clearly in the theory of thinking itself: there lies the epicenter of the disease of consciousness, and from this theory the other symptoms arise which are, in the sense we have described, of subconscious origin. Disturbed thinking means a disturbed life.

There is something disturbed about my way of life if a man calls me an idiot in a blunt or subtle way and I am "insulted" by it, that is, I feel myself to be mentally injured. Either he is right, in which case there is no reason to feel insulted, or he is wrong or knows that he is being unjust, that is, he *wants* to insult me. In this case there is just as little reason to feel insulted. I may also be unsure. *Am* I dumb? *Am* I so horrible? I, who have always thought of myself as smart and honest. . . . But in that case I should be grateful that an opportunity has finally come up to study the issue thoroughly. Despite all rational thought processes I do feel insulted, and this shows how much I can be ruled by unclear, uncontrolled mental impulses. Naturally it is also a symptom of disease on the part of the insulter that he wanted to do me mental harm.

The purpose of this chapter is to illuminate more closely what the preceding chapter only suggested: how we form the "sensitivities" of subconscious origin, mental habits, and everything that is called the subconscious. In the next chapter we shall try to show how man can work against these tendencies.

It was suggested that even psychologists have by and large succumbed to the general disease. This is evident from their habit of seeing and describing only the outside of the soul and of mental life. This is caused in part by the methods of observation deriving from natural science, and in part by a clearly recognized incapacity for introspection, for internal sight. If the very possibility of *inner* experience is doubted, then there is in fact nothing left for us to do but to observe and describe the *consequences* of mental life.

Why then is self-observation a doubtful possibility? Because, simply put, the observer and the object of observation are the same person. Everyone knows how hard it is to observe their current emotional impulses, to say nothing of deeper and more powerful drives. But for an external observer, for a psychologist or a doctor, the bridge from the observed to an understanding of the observed through inner experience is absolutely essential. We cannot directly observe the mental experiences of another person, only their external appearances; and we can, or we could understand those appearances correctly only by knowing what they meant from our own personal experience.

Psychologists or external observers have the same difficulty: it is hardly any easier for them than for patients to observe themselves, for instance, during an outburst of rage, although they may control their rage better than the patient. Nevertheless, their understanding of the patient depends on their own inner experience—with little scientific justification, because psychologists have, most likely, devoted little effort to the development of their capacity for inner observation. They are very nearly in the same condition as everyone else: for them *inner experience* remains a faint, barely guessed at, borderline state of consciousness that is unclear in comparison to the conscious clarity and sharpness of the *products* of inner life: the already thought, the already perceived. I will show by example what is meant by inner experience.

When I hear or read a word, then there is, on the one hand, a perceivable sign—acoustically or optically perceived —and, on the other, an inner activity without which the word would not work for me, that is, I would not understand it. At the very least, in the case of a language I don't know, the inner act has to take place so that I know I am hearing a word. The word has to mean something to me, at least that it *is* a word, otherwise I do not become aware of it at all. When children are learning to speak the inner act of understanding is very clearly present: this act is essential in order for what they have heard to become a word. In an adult this inner act is generally slept through, and only its result is clearly defined—the already understood word, the understood meaning—and this hides the inner experience of understanding which must be taking place, and which is quite obvious and striking in the case of children. We are already familiar with this from another standpoint: *understanding* is a process in the immediate present (presence of mind) which is superconscious for people of our day. This is why the inner experience is hardly ever experienced, and then only faintly, as if shrouded in fog.

Nevertheless, the nature of words and thoughts is such that we perform this inner act, without consciously experiencing it, each time we understand a text. It is a superconscious ability, similar to speaking, during which neither the grammar that we use, nor the formation of sounds that we carry out, is conscious. If we consider our typical emotional life we see an altogether different picture. We experience feelings as present, and at the same time independent of our conscious will; they appear and fade away without our intention, but in a correspondingly dreamlike fashion. We cannot shed light on them by a process of understanding, as we can with a thought: they only show us their outside, which exerts force on us, forces us to feel, to feel the feeling at hand. These are not cognitive feelings, about which we have only a few intuitive clues, but personal feelings. Because the inside of a feeling is closed to us, we cannot directly remember the feeling: to remember a feeling we always grasp at a *mental picture,* which we can immediately draw into consciousness, and the corresponding feeling more or less accompanies this mental picture.

All this characterizes the normal emotional life, with its unspeaking feelings that play the scale from good-for-me to bad-for-me, as a part of the subconscious. It has a similarity to the weaving of associations: associations also come and go according to *their* laws, without the conscious intention of the subject who experiences them. If many psychologies equate associating and thinking, that only shows, on the one hand, that they do not notice the inner act of understanding because they have themselves been infected by diseased consciousness. On the other hand, it also shows that most of what gets called thinking is in fact only association.

As mentioned in Chapter 1, the will is, initially, an illumined will only during concentrated, pure thinking, when we experience it as the will to think. Otherwise the experience of the will remains even more external than with thinking and feeling: what we experience is the result of the act of will. Even though I have to be very active when I will something, and am doing something on my own initiative, I do not know what I am doing and how I do it—a further example of superconscious ability. "Willing" can also combine with a feeling that comes from the subconscious; this makes will also subconscious. This does not refer to the will that carries things out, but to the will that equips a feeling with an impulse toward action. The action itself can then happen in a consciously chosen way through the superconscious will. The word subconscious does not refer to a content (content is always conscious, or we wouldn't know about it) but refers rather to the *origin* of a habit or an impulse or a feeling: the source they come from is subconscious.

Because we do not notice our inner life during understanding or thinking, the automaton model seems plausible. No one who is seriously involved with automatons or computers can, however, believe that machines have inner experiences. But a belief may well arise that man, also, has no inner experience. This leads to merely external observation and description of his mental life from the standpoint of his actions and of his production. But this aspect of humanity *can* be imitated by machines. Such imitations lead to the assertion that man behaves analogously to the machine. This is an erroneous conclusion, but hard to refute with regard to a great number of human actions because the routine, habitual part of life can in fact run on in a machinelike way.

Man could be capable of real inner experience, as we hinted at in Chapter 2, and then his mental life *would* be healthy. But this kind of experience is also absolutely necessary to *make* the mental life healthy. External proofs "that I am"—confirmations, successes, self-realizations—can only be proof for *someone*. They can only prove something for someone who already exists independently of the proofs. The proofs cannot create a subject: they presuppose a subject.

These ideas mean that the capacity for inner observation, so essential to any psychology, is not a given. Yet I know of no school of psychology or psychological training that concerns itself with these problems. Psychologists use inner observation alongside their external observation of the patient's behavior more or less according to their talents and the necessity at hand. The problem, the fact that there are these two kinds of observation, is hardly known at all. We can see the process very clearly when we think: the footsteps of thinking in the brain are easy to "see," but the being who does the walking, or the movement itself, is not experienced and often barely guessed at.

If a human being has mental problems the main cause is the lack of actual self-experience occurring in full presentness. Only a being who is unsure of its own existence can have irrational fears—and every fear, even the most reasonable, is irrational: it overburdens the subject's situation. Only such a being could be insulted or have "bad nerves" or try to solve life's difficulties by hiding them. They can be hid by drinking, getting drunk, and not only by means of alcohol or drugs or distractions but also by well-schooled, even highly esteemed means, as for example striving for success, money, and power. If someone *experiences* his own being with unshakable firmness, and also knows this being to be eternal and immortal because he experiences it independently of the body, and if he knows that nothing can touch or affect this essence unless this being allows it, then every turn of fate will be met differently than if all of this is only *thought* or if one is convinced that it is not true. In the latter case one experiences one's being as dependent on outer life, on other people's opinion, on external circumstances, and everything has to be experienced from that standpoint. How could the idea arise for such a person that life was *given* to him—*he* didn't arrange it all—so that he might help others? We can only give, only really help, only serve others, if we *are*. And man only *is* when he experiences this being in a living way. Tauler's maxim applies here: "If I were a king and did not know it, then I would not be a king."

A psychology can only be built on the basis of self-experience, which is possible for modern man. The absence of this experience is the cause and necessary precondition for the common, fundamental disease of consciousness, which in turn causes the spectrum of mental problems and diseases. It is only through a complete experience of the I-being's reality that we can turn to the phenomena of the subconscious and examine them in the well-founded hope that we will not be torn along by their power and crazed growth, which certainly happens when a man delves within, trying to observe the waves and storms of his emotions and calm them down. Most efforts to become "a better person" are just as unfruitful: who is fighting against whom? And do we really know what a better man is? This is not to object in any way to efforts to make one's behavior positive for one's surroundings. But control of our behavior should not tempt us to believe that we have really changed something in the soul. In the next chapter we will see how the reorientation of mental forces can proceed very differently from a mere struggle against bad habits, passions, or instincts. We must try to strengthen the being within, and bring it to self-experience, because that being alone is powerful enough and insightful enough to survive such a struggle. But then there would be no struggle; the mere presence, the existence of this real being *is* the victorious completion of the struggle.

The Source of Subconscious Habits

As we sketched out in Chapter 1, man's attempt to experience his inner mental activity leads him in two directions, each of which brings him to the border of his field of consciousness. In the direction of the sources of his abilities he comes to the region we called the superconscious. And if he examines his power over his own conscious life—what he can and cannot do—he comes very soon to a limit where it is clear that autonomous habits, passions and impulses work themselves into consciousness and often have a determinative influence there. These influences are felt as either desirable or undesirable and this feeling can switch back and forth with regard to a single impulse. But in each case consciousness has to admit: "There is nothing I can do about it" or in other words, "It is not I who wills it."

It is apparent without further comment that all our mental problems stem from this region. It is harder to realize that the antidote, the solution to the problems, must come from the other side, from the superconscious. Man must cultivate these superconscious powers and so shift his conscious life in the direction of liveliness and presence. This is to enrich its abilities, its power. To substantiate this insight, we will now consider the formation and the origin of the subconscious.

Small children have no mental habits and are not egotistical: the feeling of an "I" arises when they begin to address their physical bodies as "I." The process of learning to speak and think reveals a subsequently forgotten facility for attention that makes possible the first, wordless understanding. It also reveals the independence of this capacity for speaking and understanding from corporeality. Corporeality is inherited. But heredity has nothing to do with learning to speak and, therefore, with learning to think. Any child can learn any language with equal facility. If you take a child from Stuttgart to Japan before the child can speak, he or she will learn Japanese as quickly as a Japanese child and without any Swabian accent. If you take a black child from Zimbabwe to Hamburg he or she will speak Hamburgian German without any of the guttural vowel sounds of the African native tongue. And if the environment is bilingual, the child will learn both languages at once, keeping the two systems of grammar separate and flawlessly reproducing what may be two utterly different vocal systems. This is highly significant, because speaking is a physiological as well as mental event: the speech organs themselves are subject to heredity, but their functioning is not. From this we may conclude that the forces or energies needed for functioning and for imitating are *free energies*. They are not bound to corporeality, are not inherited, and are, initially, free of "habits"—for example, no particular language is imitated in preference to any other. This is characteristic of the free energies: they are forces of capability, formless, containing the possibility of making new forms. Once fastened to a form the corresponding capability is limited: think of how difficult it is to learn a second or third language later in life, an effort that is made in a very different way.

Most mentally handicapped children are physically well

built and develop well physically up to a certain age. They are remarkably healthy, often even remarkably strong in the sense that they hardly ever get tired. They cannot learn to speak, or they do so in a deficient manner. It seems appropriate to think that in these cases *free* life energies and forces of sensitivity are lacking or are insufficient.

All later capabilities—of a specifically human kind—are based on speaking and thinking. They seem to be just as conditioned by the environment as the basic human qualities: without a speaking, thinking environment, the child never learns to stand upright. Gradually, the child then learns to count, to do sums, and so on. Where does the energy come from for all this? How do the capacities develop? Certainly much that can come about later cannot be developed at an early age. These questions are valid for later phases of development as well. An eight-year-old child will hardly be able to understand or enjoy a poem by Goethe, and not because of a lack of knowledge or of intellectual understanding.

All specifically human capabilities are neither inborn (as, for instance, the ability to digest food) nor arrived at by a natural ripening (as, for instance, the ability to reproduce). They are "learned" from the human environment, and this word as we have seen has nothing to do with adult learning. The two processes of learning can be represented by the learning of the mother tongue and the later learning of another language by means of the mother tongue. At an advanced level the speaking of the foreign language becomes a matter of a feel for the language; at that point the superconscious forces take over the new language as an *ability*. These energies have always been present, more or less, during the early stages of the learning process, according to whether the student is more or less gifted. It is much the same with other human abilities, for example, with crafts or with artistic pursuits. But a small child does not yet have the energies to acquire these abilities, and even the mother tongue cannot be learned immediately after birth.

On the other hand, we see an inverse development in biological life: in this area the child or adult is more gifted with vitality the younger he or she is. Energies for growth, regeneration, and healing are not physical energies, for they always make forms, living forms: these forms are built into a mobile organism, according to its sensitivity: shying away, grasping, and so on. So we might say that the energies of growth are accompanied by instinctive energies of sensitivity. This is how it works with animals as well. In the course of human development these formative forces are freed from the human's "animal" organism. Of course this organism is not animal: it is "unfinished" at birth, so much so that without long-term support it could never stay alive. But for this very reason it is plastic and formable by outside influences. An example of this far-reaching formability is the process of learning to speak, even as a physiological achievement on the part of the speech organs, which are ready for *any* language. It is rare to successfully unlearn the sounds of the mother tongue so that they are not perceptible when the foreign language is spoken. Appropriate research confirms the evident conclusion that the freed forces of the organism are used for the learned human abilities, and this is why not everything can be learned in childhood. Obvious stepping stones in this development lie at the time of the change of teeth and at puberty, and a further marker can be guessed at, at around the age of twenty-one. The first two phases show up clearly in physical and emotional changes, the end of the third is characterized more by spiritual ripeness. Among so-called primitive peoples the attainment of the first two stages is marked by ceremonies, rites, and appropriate socialization. This corresponds among so-called civilized peoples to the beginning of the school years and to religious confirmation. The first three approximately seven-year periods do not complete the process of the liberation of life energies and energies of sensitivity. This process continues uninterruptedly until death. In later years it is more covered up. Significant points in this seven-year periodicity were more or less conscious in the course of cultural history. There is the moment, for example, when the greater part of the human body is physically changed. So it is that Dante's great adventure begins in his thirty-fifth year, "*nel mezzo del cammin di nostra vita*": "As

I stood halfway on life's path." For us it is of great importance to know that the process of the liberation of energies
in a normal human being takes place throughout life. There
is nothing similar in an animal: the animal's energies are of a
bound kind, and they are never freed in the course of life.
Therefore its development remains natural: it cannot learn,
it can only be trained, and that only at an early age. You may
say, jokingly, that something similar goes on in many
schools. The difference between instruction and animal-style
training is in fact no longer very clear.

In man, the free forces belong to the I-being. We could call
them superfluous energies. They would be superfluous for a
purely biological, instinctive being. For an I-being, they are
the means of expressing itself through a physical, living organism. The means of expression is speech: not only spoken
language, but every gesture, mimicry, smiling, crying, elo-
quent silence, glance—everything done with the intention of
expression. Speech, in this larger sense, is possessed only by
I-beings, who therefore could also be called word-beings.
Part of "speech" is that speech can be dropped: it doesn't
have to happen, it is not instinctive. It can be interrupted or
stopped altogether by second thoughts, or by an inner decision. This is generally forgotten when people talk of language
or "speaking" in animals. A being completely formed as to
his qualities, feelings, and instincts is incapable of an intentional expression or any intention at all and can have no
claim to language or to free forces, because he is completely
subject to preordained forms of feelings, reactions, and instincts. An I-being, on the other hand, who is "unfinished"
enough to express himself, must have free energies at his
command.

The I-oriented free energies are word energies: they serve
not only talking and thinking, but also cognition, creation,
and everything in the realm of the word. Whatever man
knows, says something to him; whatever he does is statement
—and not always a desired statement. Let us turn first to
knowledge, cognition. We saw in the first chapter that cognition, like everything else in the realm of words, is not a

private area, just as language and thinking are not private. Universal energies speak to the human soul through the superconscious: through the how of thinking, through cognitive feeling (e.g., the feeling of obviousness), or through cognitive will (as it comes to us during pure thinking or, during perception, in the opposite direction from our normal will, which flows from us out into the world).

These universal energies do not oblige us in any way—no more than do words that we hear: they have to be met by my acceptance—they do not force me to do anything. The newly freed energies of man are the energies of receptive cognition: they unite with whatever shines toward man from his environment. This is how man cognizes. But he is far from cognizing all of what radiates toward him. Most of it goes by unnoticed. Who can distinguish, purely by perception, between a living grain of seed and a dead one? There is a vast real difference between them, but it is not "seen." Who can experience the feelings of another person, even someone standing close by? We do not even experience our own process of thought. Everything superconscious in us remains unexperienced. We may suspect that we perceive and cognize only a fragment of the natural world as well.

Imagine a being that can only see a human's shoes. Such a being would carefully observe and measure the behavior of the shoes: at night the shoes (that is, the objects, because it would not know about men and feet and therefore it would have no concept for "shoe") are at rest. In the morning they begin to move, first in a limited area, then down the "steps" and into a "car" where they make only a few small movements. Later they move—always alternating with one in front, then the other—into a building. At night they return to the point of origin, often after some detours. All day long they are warmer than at night, most likely a result of their motion. Occasionally their outer surface comes into contact with a brush, a cloth, and a fatty substance and as a result they become more optically reflective. The being in question can build a whole science on these observations. It would measure the average distance between the shoes when in movement, ascertain the frequency with which they alternate, count the number of steps and all irregularities of movement, and form appropriate hypotheses to explain these observations. It might come to assume the existence of invisible forces that maintain a near constant distance between the two objects when they are in motion. With the objects at rest, these forces do not operate as effectively.

We could also assume a being that sees not only the shoes but the feet as well, up to the ankles, or up to the knees, or to the chest. Assume a being who sees the *whole human being: how much does a human being see of the whole human being?*

Man knows of—cognizes—only a fragment of what comes toward him from the world. What happens to that part of the light energies approaching him that he does not consciously receive? The same question can be put differently: what becomes of the energies that have been freed from organizing the body and that man does not use for cognition? It is the same question, because in regard to knowledge the distinction between inner and outer has no validity. *Where* is cognition? Cognition is a single world reality, brought into the realm of appearance by man, and it determines inner and outer. Cognition itself cannot therefore be either internal or external, and so we can handle the same question in these two different ways.

Since man is an I-being he has command, from the very start, over *free, superfluous energies.* As an I-being he has no finished form: he is teachable, not simply trainable, and he can determine his own course. Therefore reality does not have the same predetermined effect on him that it has on an animal. Animals behave according to type: they react to the environment and to circumstances. Man does not react, if he is behaving in *human* fashion: instead, he perceives, considers, and decides. In the animal, "perception" (which is not perception in the human sense) leads seamlessly into "action" (which is not action in the human sense). Man can *think* after perceiving. In general, man does not *have* to: he *can,* because he has superfluous energies with which to cognize and make new beginnings.

Because he has no completely formed, closed-off character,

because he has free energies, he also is faced with the problem of what to do with these energies that increase throughout his life. Or to put it in other terms, what that part of reality he does not consciously perceive will do with *him*. This problem was solved by early mankind through traditional paths, cults, religions, membership in communities, for example, the initiatic rites by which youths were taken into the society of adult men. The superfluous energies were not felt as *one's own*, there was no sense that one brought forth one's own thoughts, and apart from a few chosen ones, no one said (and no one could say) "I think" or even "I." Energies for thinking and cognizing were felt to be superhuman or divine. Therefore they could be kept under control by "religion," which pulsed through all lived experience. The energies themselves *were* the reality of religion, which was not something special alongside the reality of life, but was the very kernel of reality. In the age of the consciousness-soul, in which we now live, nearly everything traditional that could be effective as a means of controlling this problem has been lost. Man says "I," "I think"; he has to deal with his free energies on his own. Or we could say he carries the responsibility for the effects of the world energies that stream toward him of which he is not conscious.

We can find another analogy between early man and childhood. In both cases *habits,* inspired habits, are formed. In the one case religious, cult, traditional customs, social usages; among children similar habits but also those considered healthy by the environment for order, cleanliness, and obedience. In later ages, either of humanity or of the individual, new measures are necessary to realize the possibilities opened up by the new energies. We have seen, for example, that the great possibility of conscious experience of presence, the true, the real experience of the *I,* is widely rejected today, and we have considered in part the consequences of such an attitude. These can all be summed up as follows: instead of an experience of the *I,* egotism rules individual life and the life of mankind.

We can characterize the *I* and the essence of egotism in an unusual way if we compare them with regard to the strength of their *being*. Such comparison shows that the ego is a very weak *I*. The strength or intensity of existence during I-experience reveals itself in that the *I* can surrender itself to something, and the more it does so, the more self-forgetful it becomes. That is, the more strongly and intensively the *I* exists, the more undivided its awareness. The I-being is not a static being but exists in self-surrender. You might be of the opinion that the I-being, therefore, is at its strongest in a child, with the child's practically unlimited capacity to learn the fundamental functions of consciousness by means of devoted attention. This would merely be a half-truth. The essence of a child is in fact nearly unclouded: that is, nearly unexposed to the distracting influences that rise up from the adult's subconscious. But children are not capable of experiencing themselves, just because they live *entirely* in self-surrender. Man can achieve self-experience *in the midst of surrender* only though exercises of his consciousness (see Chapter 5), but first he has to go through a period of egotism. Self-experience begins in egotism as self-feeling, and so the detour through egotism is unavoidable. The danger is that man will never find a way out of egotism. In egotism the awareness is split between world and organism, so that experience of one's own organism becomes the seed of self-feeling. Because egotism is a weak, shadowy self-feeling, bound up with past consciousness, it continually requires "confirmations," and these confirmations are what destroy both individual and social life.

The environment attempts to inculcate habits in the child which are, on the one hand, transparently clear and consciously justified (perhaps by means of a religious consciousness). On the other hand, the habits and modes of behavior are such that neither children nor adults would have to be ashamed of themselves, or rather (as we must immediately restrict the statement) such that no one of two hundred years ago would have to be ashamed. In the meantime, many habitual activities for which one would then have been ashamed have become quite acceptable in the best homes, and people are even proud of some of them, thanks in part to the "enlightening" activity of the so-called sciences of anthropology and psychology.

Egotism

The *I* gives, the ego takes. The destructiveness of the ego is immediately evident in social terms: *everyone* wants to take, to have, and the result is discord and warfare. Today we are experiencing the collapse of a social system based on egotism both in the East and in the West. Long ago the fanatic belief of economic liberalism (that if the individual strives for maximum economic prosperity the result will be maximum prosperity for all) has been shown to be wishful thinking, an ideology meant to somehow socially justify gross egotism. The answer to liberalism was hardly better. Marx never discovered that individual egotism cannot be overcome through class egotism. Class egotism, national egotism, or the egotism of the individual: they all lead to a general defeat in a war of all against all. No social contract helps here. An agreement as to the socially necessary limits on egotism is as ineffective as an agreement on *Realpolitik* as a basis for marriage. Ambition against ambition, greed against greed, will-to-power against will-to-power—how can this lead anywhere but to continual conflict?

Egotism is not only socially destructive; it is also a disease for the individual. Man has the use of free word energies. It would be healthy for him to use these *as* word energies, that is, a healthy life would be a creative life. Not everyone has to be a poet, sculptor, or scientist: everyone is creative who radiates peace and the warmth of love and evokes these in others. Such people, mostly quite unknown women and men —not artists, not "personalities"—are the real helpers of mankind. Tolstoy, in *War and Peace,* portrayed such a person in the figure of the simple soldier, Platon Karatyev. Fame and renown are often a hindrance to creative abilities.

Egotism means that one's attention is divided: a large portion is directed to oneself, to the effect and consequences of one's activity, and not to the activity itself, the matter at hand. Stage fright is a typical symptom: artists or lecturers are concerned with themselves—will it go well? will it be a success?—and not with their work. And for this very reason the work fares badly as well. Creativity is possible only in a state of concentration: loose, uncramped, but concentrated. Everything that disturbs the concentration detracts from creativity. Awareness is man himself, it is the *I*. If man is concerned with himself, as in egotism, he cannot realize his healthy, creative existence. And creation is a pleasure: the greatest of all pleasures.

Egotism always has pretensions, desires, and longings. These repeat themselves and do not really want to be satisfied permanently. Desire itself is a confirmation that I exist, and every normal feeling, even feelings of suffering, are self-confirmations. We would rather suffer than have no feelings at all. Unsatisfied desires seem bad to us, but satisfaction when it comes lasts at most only a short time and is really *meant* to last only a short time. The repetitive nature of desires, the attachment to one form of sensation, show how *unwordlike* they are: they seek nothing new (a bar of chocolate always offers the same taste). What is animal-like in man (animals themselves have no harmful desires) is shown in repetition compulsion.

The word selfishness expresses the essence of egotism: man searches for his own *self*, but he will never find it by gratifying selfish desires. But life and the functions of the soul are made to serve this Danaid labor (the Danaids poured water into a leaky vessel). Even the most luminous function of the soul, thinking, gets taken over: it too can be in the service of self feeling. It discovers ever-new varieties of self-feeling in the body and the mind.

We will not deal now with the details of the physical forms of self-feeling, but we will stress one point: the body has only purely biological needs: it has no desire, no lust. It has hunger and thirst, but no gourmet taste buds: just like a wild animal, which would never prolong its hunger or push away food in order to be able to have a taste of something more delicious later on. Animals have no pleasure-seeking personal habits: I have yet to see a cigar-smoking hedgehog.

Feelings of pleasure and the need for pleasure come from the mind; the body is merely their instrument. When priests demonstrate against celibacy in the name of the "proven needs of the body" they only demonstrate their confusion: lust belongs not to the body, but to the mind. The body has no feelings. Our feeling nature is at the heart of egotism: for selfishness strives after self-feeling in lieu of the self-experience or self-cognition it has rejected. If the self-experience of consciousness of the soul were to become as intensive as our tactile experience of physical objects, then selfishness would be unnecessary, and it would in fact not exist. Feeling feels no *thing,* as we have said before: it feels itself, uncognitively, and is at the same time beyond the reach of the autonomy of consciousness: feeling comes and goes by its own power. The subconscious nature of this process reveals itself in just this way, and it is related in this regard to association. In fact, feelings are often coupled to associative elements. This accounts for the possibility of learning about a person's feeling life by paying attention to his or her associations as they appear in language and thought.

Self-feeling feelings are not necessarily directed to man's bodily instrument. There are purely mental forms of selfish self-confirmation, such as the aforementioned ambition, envy, greed, and an unlimited number of other habits, which have no generally accepted names. One of these would be justifiable anger, boiling internally against a person or a group; this is often a source of mental lust. The rage, often quite silent, against the stupidity or vileness of others is also a pleasure—we willingly engage in it. Just as we say much more about evil and immorality in others than we do about nobility and morality. If you observe a group of chattering men or women and calculate the statistics, you will see how unevenly they distribute good and evil to their fellow humans.

All forms of self-seeking are necessarily linked to dishonesty, and above all to dishonesty with oneself. Even though much of what was once shameful has become an object of pride, this attitude is largely a front: when dealing with others we always remain on our best behavior. Dishonesty toward oneself is the source of the unbelievable quantity of dishonesty that circulates in society. Often dishonesty is organized and cultivated by society, separating men from one another like a thick fog and spoiling every attempt to understand one another.

The various forms of egotism have a common trait. They reduce the achievements of the individual, even when this goes unnoticed. *Lack of self-trust* is one negative form of this, and those who suffer from it are obviously hindered in their actions, even when they have good intuitions about what is to be done. Ambition is not always considered a negative quality, but it is socially as well as individually harmful, because it places people in inappropriately high positions in which they are bound to fail. Whether their incompetence is noticed or remains hidden does not matter, and much effort, time, and energy is spent in the effort to conceal it. *Feelings of inferiority* and overcompensation for the same are as widely spread as envy, greed, and "oversensitivity," all of which tend to relate to and judge everything with regard to one's self. It is certainly desirable to have an agreeable career, but the reliance on one's career as a means of bringing about feelings of success quickly leads a person to a situation in which his activity is falsely understood, being oriented toward success rather than toward work. It is important and beautiful to help others through our work—as a doctor, priest, teacher, and so on—or outside of the workplace. But when it becomes more important that *I* help someone than that he *be* helped, then my helping loses both its moral significance and its practical usefulness. I am no longer able to judge objectively what ought to be done. Often helping is used to stimulate dependencies, but why? All such methods of relating to one another bring us away from reality, away from cognition and away from a right judgment of what is happening. And they are all *unwanted:* no one decides to be

75

envious or to feel his inferiority or to be "oversensitive" like a mimosa.

No one decides to be an egotist, and, once an egotist, it is hard to stop being one despite all virtuous resolutions. Egotism is a *subconscious* form, unwanted, often lived through with internal resistance, and all its myriad forms, shifting into one another and mutually interdependent, are of subconscious, opaque origin. And we can also ascertain the reverse: all subconsciously based forms of behavior stand under the sign of egotism.

Ever since Stirner and Nietzsche there have been philosophers of egotism again and again, by which no slight is intended against the genius and upright intentions of either of these men. Today most psychologists claim that man is fundamentally egotistical, as we have already considered at some length. But we should not forget, and this points to the possible cure for our common disease of consciousness, that this opinion is itself the result of an act of cognition! If man were egotistical through and through, he would never notice it (just as those who see only blue could have no knowledge of blue): he would never be able to form the concept of egotism if he were only familiar with egotistical behavior. What would egotism mean to him? Egotism *is* discovered; the authority within that makes this discovery, our center of cognition, is certainly not egotistical itself, or it would never have made this discovery. Egotism is not native with us; it is a necessary stepping-stone to experience of the *I*. It sets man on his own two feet so that he can walk on his own: so that he can go from being a taker to being a giver and find his way from solitude to his fellow man. It is a matter of human freedom whether we take this step or remain in the condition into which we have fallen without choice and without conscious decision—a condition where the products of the subconscious are dominant, but where we have also *discovered* and formulated them. From this peculiar circumstance alone —the fact that our situation has been formulated consciously —we could draw the conclusion that the subconscious is not coercive, and that the possibility of overcoming it does exist.

It is a philosophy of egotism that results in the thought

that in nature a struggle for existence rules all and directs "evolution." This thought is quite time-bound: it stems from the era and from the outlook of economic liberalism. It is anthropomorphic through and through. But only today are we learning to value properly the natural, biological equilibrium present in nature when man does not interfere destructively. There is no normal, "natural struggle" in nature, no "evolutionary impulse," no "fight." And this is not only because the idea of a fight is hard to justify by observation— like the idea of helping, of which there might appear to be just as many examples—there is not even historical evidence for the survival of the fittest. When a catastrophe limits the food supply, it is by no means the strongest who survive, but often the least imposing, smallest species and the least imposing individual within them. Becoming *smaller* is a more widespread phenomenon in paleontology than becoming fit. What would fitness mean in nature? If we can't answer this question clearly, then the statement that the fit survive is nonsense: it means that the survivor is more fit, which is no more than to say that "the survivor is the survivor." Seen biologically, man would have to rank as the most unfit of all creatures in nature. Darwin's thought obviously stems from the struggle for economic superiority. In what sense the winner of *this* struggle can be called the most fit is another question—and an impolite one.

We can try to justify our egotistical habits and ways of life ideologically, but the speaker in us, the word-being, will always be ashamed of these modes of conduct. On the surface it is possible to be proud of our recklessness, unsentimentality, pitilessness, hardness, manliness. There are and have been so-called worldviews that cherished and cultivated these qualities. But they do not think the thought through to the end, and within the family, among members of the same belief system, no one behaves according to such views. A simple story can illuminate the nature of egotism and altruism.

Hell is a place where there is plenty of soup for the inmates, but the spoons have such long handles that no one can bring food to his or her mouth. The sufferings of these hungry sinners in front of the pot full of soup are unspeakable. And how is it in heaven? There we find the same situation: Plenty of soup, spoons with oversize handles. But in heaven the inmates have hit on the idea that they can feed each other, reaching the spoon not to their own mouths but to the mouths of their neighbors. Selflessness feeds them amply.

The Formation of the Subconscious

Egotism appears in very pronounced form in the men and women of today. We will not concern ourselves with its origin; that lies beyond the scope of the present volume. But we can understand that neither an individual child nor humanity as a whole could arrive at an experience of the *I* if there were no detour through egotism. Everything having to do with egotism separates man from the superconscious: in this way, he could become independent of the superconscious. Why is it necessary for him to be free in his cognizing or creating? Everybody has moments when he or she experiences freedom immediately, and everybody comes into other situations in life and faces his or her own unfreedom. Unfreedom does not come from any physical, biological determination, but from the alienated portion of the soul that we have come to know as the subconscious. The already mentioned vague, opaque feelings, impulses, and associations which can prevail, often successfully, against our conscious will, all come from this portion of the soul. Sometimes consciousness places itself on the side of these impulses, justifies them in thought, and behaves as if everything were taking place according to well-considered, free decisions.

Autonomous attention is *form free*, that is, it is not formed in advance. It can assume any form temporarily, can identify with anything and then release itself from the form it has taken and turn toward some new object. Preformed mental constructions are, as a matter of course, noncognitive for the very reason that they are already permanently formed and fixed. Nothing can be cognized out of egotism; every cognition is selfless, or it is not cognition at all. Selfishness and cognition are opposite. When one is preoccupied with one's *self*, one cannot find what there is to cognize.

Premade forms are useless for the creation of new forms, or for creativity in general: the new can only arise from what is form free. For real speaking—when something new gets said—there must be a wordless capacity to conceive of this newness. Then it is poured into a language made up of words, and it is still fluid, not yet fixed. The already formed does not speak; or it does so only if some understanding, or some understander, lifts the preformed words, a written text for example, back into the fluid phase. Only in this way can it do its "wording" and be understood. We recognized improvisation as the primary creative, innovative gesture. This gesture stands diametrically opposed to subconscious forms, associations, and everything habitual. We could contrast two groups of characteristics:

SUBCONSCIOUS	SUPERCONSCIOUS
finished	unfinished
habit	capacity
repetition	improvisation
preformed	form free
association	thinking
emotion	feeling
instinct	I will it

The left-hand column plays a far greater role in human life than the right-hand column. Yet all that is specifically human is to be found in the right-hand column. Even the individual elements on the left have their origin in the sphere from which the others come. No ego without an *I*; no subconscious that does not owe its existence to the superconscious. Human life, with its colorful joys and sufferings, plays itself out between the two boundaries that are our only direct experience of the superconscious and the subconscious.

Catullus' distich beautifully describes the character of a subconscious impulse:

Odi et amo. Quare id faciam, fortasse requiris.
  Nescio. Sed fieri sentio et excrucior.

I hate and I love. You may well ask me why.
I do not know. But so it is; I feel it and pain crucifies me.

Nescio: I do not know. Catullus points with this word to the subconscious origin of his double feeling, and the beauty of the poem lies in just this activity of pointing, which constitutes the whole of the poem. It is the process of becoming conscious that lifts the poem free from the condition of mere suffering: for the moment of the poem's creation, consciousness rises out of the feeling and sees itself, sees the feeling, sees the state of the soul, and describes all this: it is full of verbs, full of activity, of process (eight verbs in a total of fourteen words). A kind of daring lies at the axis of the poem: *nescio,* I do not know.

How does the subconscious, indicated by the word *nescio,* get formed? We have to look for the origin of mental forms: why and where did the first mental form come about?

The child learns to speak and also, therefore, to think, before he can say "I." At first, the child speaks of his physical appearance, which for an adult is the whole child, in the third or second person: "Peter is going outside," or, "You are going outside." Both for the child and for humanity, speaking is preindividual. After a certain time this physical appearance is referred to in the first person: "I am going outside." The child's adult environment generally misunderstands this highly intuitive process. As we have seen (Section 1.3) this is in fact an intuitive process: "I" and "you" cannot be explained. We can draw two important conclusions from the two forms of address toward one's own body. The child can already speak quite well, yet he or she does not say "I," or not in the correct sense. The speaker is still "outside of the body," has not yet identified with the body. On the other hand, it cannot yet say "I," cannot succeed in the intuition of the "I" before this identification has taken place. That is to say, the speaker cannot experience itself as an *I* before this identification. Does the *I*, the speaker, really become the body at this point? Not at all. What takes place by means of this identification is the formation of the ego: *this is what feels itself to be* identical with the body.

The *I* finds in the body a mirror: it beholds its own mirror image and says "I" to it. The *I* itself, the speaker—not to be confused with the apparatus, the loudspeaker—remains invisible, unlocalizable, and superconscious to itself, unable to be experienced. The ego, the I-feeling, arises because the knowing, speaking *I* has identified itself with a *form*. This is an already given form: not only as a physical body, but as a living and sensitive body, a growing, moving, sentient corporeality. An animal can move of its own accord because it is a sentient creature, and its movements are meaningful, guided by sensations. An animal can shy away or snap at something, sometimes even very accurately as birds do with their beaks. Compare this ability with the growth and the externally caused movement of plants. Even the active species of plants, such as the mimosa or the Venus flytrap, exhibit a more mechanical movement than is the case with animals. The child identifies with a physical form, a form made of creative forces, and a form of sensitivity. One could speak of three corresponding "bodies" if by body one means merely something formed. The form of sensitivity contains all the reflexes, all the "feelings" that direct the inner movements of the adult and remain unconscious, until the corresponding life functions become diseased.

The essence of the subconscious would therefore be egoic feeling, a kind of "I"-feeling in which *I* experiences itself not by itself, but by feeling the body. This central ego-feeling gives rise to all subsequent forms of sensitivity and desire—always egotistic and self-concerned—all habits, emotions and human instincts. How do they come about?

We have seen (Section 3.2) how forces are freed from the living, sensitive organism as it matures—forces that had previously been active in its growth, organization, and the creation of forms. They become the specifically human abilities which, characteristically, are neither inborn nor naturally developmental but come about through the effect of a human environment and then remain "free," capable of change and development. They become energies of cognition, creative energies, energies of *human* labor, which is always a *spiritual* labor, because the hands or the body are led by the spirit: Man *knows* what he labors at, or should know. With his hands he gives a form to the idea, to the word. Thus, human labor belongs to man's "word." As a result of modern technological development, this characteristic of labor is continually perverted and tends to disappear. We will return to this question later.

We have seen that, besides the freed energies that flow into human activities and make these possible, other energies always go unused. Earlier, these were explained in terms of religious cult, morality, and traditional customs. They therefore fit within an order appropriate to the individual and also to the human society. Now, in the age of the consciousness-soul, with the triumph of natural science and of a technology based on the views of such a science, traditional methods are no longer appropriate to bring order to the "superfluous" life energies and sentient energies. We must manage these energies for ourselves, and bring them under the direction of the I-being that controls all free energies so as to articulate and express itself through a body. The individual must use these energies for cognition and creation, as improvisational energies of freedom, of the word.

Experience shows that this occurs rarely. Science is still far from discovering these relationships and for several reasons the majority of people do not recognize the value of Rudolf Steiner's spiritual science, which considers these phenomena in depth. Spiritual science can be thought of as a way to answer the question, *what should be done with freed human energies in our era?*

If the energies, as they become free, are not directed either in traditional ways or in the service of the I-being, then they give rise to unfree, already formed clusters of bound energy, the forms of the subconscious. From the forces of light that go unused the realm of the soul's darkness arises. We could call this process a theft of the light energies. Earlier people spoke of this as a demonic theft. The rightful possession of the I-being falls into the service of the destructive, antihuman power of egotism. There is nothing primal about the subconscious: it originates in the highest, unused energies of man, just as in the traditional image hell is peopled with fallen *angels*. Creative energies cannot remain uncontrolled; if man does not take them in hand, they spoil. They slip into a form which is always inimical to the *I*-being, the word-being. Such finished forms are not "wordlike;" they do not *say* anything, they do not serve human expression, the expression and life of a conscious *I*. That they can be considered as belonging to man, or as man himself, by a science that knows nothing of man's essence (as is proved by its "fruits") is the symptom of a diseased consciousness. The method of infection is itself a symptom, showing the hideous strength of the subconscious: it justifies itself scientifically

The ability most misused by man is speech. Speech should serve to unite men, who have been separated by their consciousness, in a free fashion (we have already seen that words tend to leave us free) so that man can use speech *if he has something to say.* We may be amazed when children, learning to speak, use their new ability creatively, with a pure joy. Compare this to gossip, an apparently harmless form of *misused* speech. There is a certain pleasure in gossip as well. But it is of a quality different from the child's joy in speaking: it delights in self-feeling during gossip and the joy is increased by its content. Gossip says: "Look how much I know, how well informed I am, how clever, how good, how witty." And there is also a lust in speaking about the weaknesses of other people. *This* pleasure has to do neither with the ability to speak nor with that which is spoken: it is a purely egotistical pleasure. Gossip must go on: we don't feel right if silence descends on a group of people. Was it always this way? The history of gossip has yet to be written: it does not stretch back very far in time.

The habit of gossip leads to many untruths, and these engender and give birth to further untruths. And so the word itself, our bridge to other men, is used as a nonword, as a token, like a card in a card game. This cheapens the value of words, just as the value of money sinks as a result of counterfeit currency. Man sins with and against the word, above all else.

Thus speech, an interhuman function, is changed to selfishness or, more exactly, to a process that does not help us either to speak or to be spoken to, but simply prepares pleasurable egotistical feelings for the speaker. An even more drastic transformation can be seen in what has been understood by the word love. For most people a love like that of Novalis—as is found in children or young people during their first romance—changes into something that has almost nothing to do with this: it is a downward metamorphosis.

Subconscious feeling forms, bound up with a corresponding will impulse, appear coercive in consciousness, in constrast to cognitive and moral intuitions, which are not only noncoercive, but often require great effort of will to be put into practice. You may be familiar with St. Paul's sigh in Romans 7:18-20, "[F]or to will is present with me; but how to perform that which is good I find not. For the good that I would I do not: but the evil which I would not, that I do. Now if I do that I would not, it is no more I that do it, but sin that dwelleth in me." He looks on at the unconscious coercions in his soul, at sin that is not merely abstract, but an individual power. St. Paul was a forerunner of later mental styles, and he *sees* this, just as he also touches the upper boundary of the soul (Galatians 2:20): "[N]evertheless I live; yet not I, but Christ liveth in me." At the upper limit of consciousness, he feels the logos-being who gives rise to the capacities of love and knowledge. He himself, the observer of all this, is the third person between these two limit cases.

Gossip generally concerns the insufficiency of other people, not of those present. The media are similar. Journalists hunt sensations, a word that means feelings. These occur almost exclusively in the area of human weaknesses such as death, crimes, and so on. Readers want this kind of sensation. Only a fraction of our newspapers would be sold if, instead of murder, rape, robbery, and deceit, they reported good deeds,

84

gentleness, moral conduct, and patience. The headline, NOTHING BAD HAPPENED TODAY would not interest most readers. Imagine a newspaper that reported good events instead of bad: who would read it?

All this is another misuse of the word. It has become a kind of lust, for most of us, to be informed about wrongdoing. Why should it interest me that in a small village near here a man and his wife and children . . . ? Or that an employee, secretly, . . . ? This fascinates the average reader so much that he mentions it the next day to all and sundry with much mental smacking-of-the-lips: "how frightful, how sneaky . . . !" The lust or pleasure in evil spreads: a precursor and substitute for one's own wrongdoing.

Almost everyone is familiar with the phenomenon of unrequited love or love that, for a variety of reasons, does not lead to a "happy end." If this becomes a conscious focus, then energies of feeling are released (this can also occur because of the death of a beloved friend) and the freed energies can take several paths. One can become ill because of the disappointment or lack of success, either mentally or physically. The mental "wound" can lead to depression, breakdown, even to suicide. The most famous example is certainly Goethe's hero Werther. Yet, as is well known, there exists another possible reaction to one's grief: the lover begins to write poems or to paint or compose music in the midst of his or her suffering and pain. In this case the freed energies do not turn into disease but change instead into creative forces. Many good poems have come from love pains or from other kinds of suffering (many bad poems as well, of course) and the gift to write may last only until the poet finds a happier love. Werther's story combines both possibilities: Goethe himself poured his pain into the novel so that his hero, not he, would commit suicide. Goethe lived on. The novel does not simply reflect an "abreaction" despite all its quaint, antiquated traits. It enjoyed an unheard of success and had a deep emotional effect on its readers. Apparently there were many unhappy love stories at that time which were taken very seriously. The course of this unhappy love shows very clearly what can be done with freed emotional energies. They can form themselves into illness; they can transform themselves through the *I* into free, creative energies.

There are infinite varieties of subconscious feeling forms. New kinds arise continually, each more distant than the last from the original energies. Light distractions are an example of the way in which these energies can be perverted: the more passive they are, the more they arouse addiction and dependence as, for example, the radio in comparison with the book, television in comparison with the radio, a spy thriller in comparison with Thomas Mann, or movies in comparison with the theater. What can only be guessed at in the theater, because of the limitations of the stage, can be *shown* in a film, where one's own active imagination and cocreativity are "spared." A special source of egotistical lust is the indulgence in a feeling of one's own flaws. This can even appear very moral: one confesses one's weaknesses; one admits them to be true. And with this admission one imagines one will escape responsibility. "I am so weak, there's nothing I can do about it. But it's good, at least, that I realize it." *Really* experiencing and knowing one's own weaknesses requires enormous strength: only a very strong person can really see and admit his weakness. A weak person must first be strengthened before he can bear to face his own weaknesses.

If a human's mental life consisted only in opaque, unconsidered habits, feeling forms, and reaction patterns, then he would be inaccessible to any new experience. He would try to avoid new things or to force all that is new into the form of the old. It is clear that in an extreme form this attitude is destructive and self-destructive. Such a soul gives the I-being, with its freedom from form and its tendency to dissolve all events, no avenue to express itself through the body. Many psychologies assume that, besides an instinct for pleasure, a death drive also plays a role in the life of the soul. These self-destructive drives are the same formations of egotism, but in their final phases.

When the energies take a fixed form they lose their word character. The already formed cannot be a source; it can neither speak nor cognize; it can only be repeated. Speech requires both an ability to say anything at all, and also an ability to understand what is said by others, to become identical with their speech intention. Both can come about only by means of free ability, not through habits. The whole sphere of subconscious form is picturable; in a certain sense it can be reckoned with and automatically reproduced. This serves as the basis of psychology. Man as robot, as automaton, comes to light as the *finished* aspect of man. Man is widely considered in scientific and (even more so) in pseudo-scientific circles to be a very complicated automaton. We can say that this claim is justified with regard to the subconscious sphere; even if it is oversimplified. Yet this sphere is not original, but comes from the missed opportunity to take up the energies locked in the subconscious and to use them freely and creatively.

The self-freeing energies can be considered superfluous, excess energies. This term distinguishes the energies absolutely necessary for biological life from the extra energies that become available to man in the course of his life. What do we actually do with these energies? Always something "superfluous." This is how we could consider all art and culture and pure cognition ("useless" in its first moments) when we compare it to animal life. Similarly superfluous is everything that serves human coziness, distraction, luxury, and low forms of pleasure. And this latter superfluity has gradually, in the course of history, come to more and more outweigh the first group of activities.

Both groups are specifically human: neither shows up in the animal kingdom. The "sphere of comforts," as we can call everything that serves self-feeling, overgrows and dominates human life among the civilized peoples and clearly serves egotism. It trains humans in pretensions and desires that are not only foreign but hostile to biological health. Even politics and international conflicts are largely determined by this sphere, through the economy or through fears regarding the economy, and it is unprofitable, in the long run, for all of us. Many people know of this excess yet nothing is done about it, because the economy already relies to a great extent on this field and no one dares to endanger its stability by sacrifices in this area.

The sphere of comforts is based on man's subconscious impulses, in other words, on egotism. Egotism does not want to say and give; it wants to have and enjoy. Thus, the distinction between the two spheres of excess can be formulated in regard to their word likeness. Culture, art, and cognition are word activities; through them the word nature of the world comes to light. Activities and phenomena in the sphere of comforts do not take this same direction: in the background there lies an ideology hostile to words, which regards man as anything but a word-being.

Animals have no superfluous or excess energies, no habits, no unhealthy desires, and no abilities that are not either inborn or given as a matter of course in their growth. In contrast to this, man's individual and collective problems come about through superfluous energies when these energies degenerate into subconscious, egotistical habits. The fundamental principle of mental health and psychological healing is to seek, therefore, other possible directions in which to live out these energies. The central question here must be: how can excess energies that have become frozen in fixed forms be freed and taken up by the I-being as creative forces?

Half-Free Energies

The *I*'s cognitive energies and the energies trapped in mental forms represent two extreme cases. In between there lies a whole continuum that we could call either not quite fixed forms or (from the opposite perspective) not quite free energies, since they emerge more or less fixedly, although their context may vary. They are not yet altogether subject to the *I*. It is characteristic of these energies that whatever they may produce always contains elements of self-feeling. Someone is helpful, but with a self-feeling egotistical pleasure in helping. Someone cognizes, but the cognition has elements of pride or gluttony. These energies, neither fully formed nor fully controlled by the *I*, have a special tendency toward resonance: they eagerly assume (resonate) the mood, desires, or opinions of another person. With the help of these energies, we behave according to how the other person woud like to see us behave. Because this kind of resonance is generally present in both parties, it tends to become mutually magnified.

Clearly this ability to resonate implies an ability to *imitate*, including the imitation of qualities that are not actually present, particularly the pretense of spiritual interests, abilities, and sensitivities. Naturally this "spirituality" has a self-feeling, egotistical character. It is an *as if,* which may nevertheless play a positive role, particularly in art. It can change into real interests and abilities. Sentimentality should also be considered an imitation of true feeling. The easy resonations of feeling during flirtation are, similarly, an imitation of love.

When these fluttering, half-free feelings have their way, the resulting behavior is characterized by a lack of continuity. A person may become involved in something that has no connection with the rest of his or her life, and often stands in sharp contradiction to it. Past and future do not exist for these forces. Yet they are not forces of presentness: they deal with the temporal present only, not the essential present. As sentimental energies they often cling to relics and mementoes. Because they are not I-energies, they either have nothing to do with words or are actually hostile to the realm of words. Therefore, when someone tells what he or she has done under their influence, the story is either hilariously funny or monstrous, with uncanny overtones. We can also look at them as transitional energies: free as to content but subconscious in style, they are the transition to subconscious formations.

For "normal" people, gaps in consciousness are the dangerous moments, the points of entry, for these energies. At such moments wakeful consciousness is partially dimmed in a particular field. Such gaps occur through mental agitation, excessive strain, tiredness (which is often a symptom itself) or by experiencing situations in which one is not in agreement, or not wholly in agreement. Often someone will *will-*

ingly open such gaps by relying on a person, authority, institution, or method that is not thoroughly understood, instead of on one's own judgment. When we go to astrologers, seers, or soothsayers, or use the various superstitious methods of guessing the future, determining favorable or unfavorable moments for our actions—all are ways of answering the question, "Who am I?" by relying on a fact, on past knowledge, instead of by trusting one's own ability to make new beginnings and to take action on one's own. Quite apart from what the horoscope may contain, the relationship to the astrologer is itself an opening up of consciousness to the influence of resonant half-free energies. And this relationship comes about in the first place only thanks to such influence. No one gets drunk in a bar or in a nightclub; we are already drunk by the time we go in to drink.

When these energies are more prevalent, the personality is characterized by an unusual instability and lack of thoroughness in its dealings and in the conduct of life. Only the temporal present counts, as if there were no access to memory at all. If the energies are active even more intensively and permanently, then we have a case of atavistic souls with atavistic abilities: clairsentience and other feelings that are often misinterpreted because the individual's thinking does not correspond to his or her feeling and the *I* takes no part in the process of cognition. These energies were once really cognitive forces, but they were under the protection of the gods and of holy institutions. Released by the gods, and not yet taken up consciously by man, they became energies of temptation, just like those in the realm of fixed mental forms. As the power of half-free energies over a person increases, the result is psychosis. The stages we have mentioned in the progressive control by these forces are part of a whole continuum. And, like everything in the soul, these half-free forces are connected with other areas: they often act in the service of subconscious forms, furthering their impulses and realizing their goals.

4

THE HEALTH

OF THE SOUL

Lyric Generalities

In the preceding chapters, we had to sketch a disheartening picture of the soul, of the normal condition of our consciousness. This chapter, along with Chapter 5, represents the more practical part of the book and must begin with a mention of what one *cannot* do (and should not try to do) with regard to problems of the soul: one should not try to attack them directly, consider them, analyze them, or take direct measures against them. This would constitute a false direction, and it would only make the problems more difficult and more acute.

These problems are a sign that the autonomous human being has become weak. If it were otherwise, if the autonomous human—capable of orienting his attention at will—were really in control of his own self, then these problems would not come up, or at least they would not be overpowering and one could live with them in peace. When the autonomous authority is weak, when the problems are there in full force, then there is no one present with sufficient independence to take these difficulties in hand. Any attention devoted to them, in the absence of the proper autonomy, would be quickly taken over by the separate impulses of the soul, that is, by the problems themselves, and it would thus become one of the symptoms: the situation would only deteriorate.

If someone has bad nerves and worries about it, his nerves get worse. And if he sees this taking place, they get even worse. Because the disease consists of the lack of autonomy, man cannot work with it in the area of the diseased functions of the soul. He must seek out an area where he is still autonomous enough so that by exercising his autonomous abilities and his capacity for attention, he can increase these faculties. As his autonomy increases, he can reasonably hope to deal with his problems and difficulties. As we saw in the first chapter, attention is the sign and the measure of mental autonomy: the autonomous being expresses itself through this very faculty of attention. If a person can intentionally direct an intensive, lasting attention toward a theme that does *not* interest him, then he is strongly autonomous. If he cannot, his autonomy is weak.

This line of thought illustrates a general principle of mental health that we could call the principle of the *indirect method*. Something is done in an area of relative strength in order to later achieve health in an area of weakness.

We might wonder why we should do anything at all about mental hygiene. Our grandparents and great-grandparents didn't bother about it and yet they were healthy, active people. The answer lies in the question. Our grandparents were *healthy*, even mentally healthy—at least, healthier than we are. We all have more or less diseased consciousnesses, and we live in an equally sick environment, surrounded by other sufferers. All this is under the control of the disease, which we have variously referred to as egotism, the forgetting of presentness, or the insurgence of subconscious forms. Even a healthy person would quickly become infected in such an environment, because he would have to adjust to the diseased lifestyles around him. And someone who knows nothing about the disease, or refuses to acquire such knowledge, is not, for that reason, any healthier. In these circumstances, something has to be actively done about our health. And yet we can still ask why it is that our grandparents had healthier stable consciousnesses.

I would like to pose a counterquestion. What is your experience of the major holidays? Consider Sunday, for example. Is that a Sun-Day for you, does it have its special solemnity? Or is it simply a day off from work, like most people's Saturday? And how do you feel about Christmas? Apart from the sentimentality that may accompany this event, does it really have any significance for you above and beyond the giving and receiving of gifts? More particularly, how do you experience Easter or Pentecost? These holidays once had a definite and individual character. Most people today have no real holidays anymore. Their life consists of workdays and days off from work, and even family occasions have lost their meaning. Does this have anything to do with mental health?

Holidays gave life a rhythm by lifting consciousness out of its everyday concerns. The felt experience of holidays was not sentimentality, which is a substitute for real feeling, but a differentiated experience analogous to our intuitions and yet rooted in a more universal, collective human experience. Attention was turned in a religious or simply human fashion toward the divine. We could also say that the center of balance of consciousness shifted upward, in the direction of the superconscious, which joins the individual with general humanity, the source of language and of thinking. The experience of holidays was just *one* of the traditional methods or arrangements for maintaining order among the self-freeing, superconscious energies that today become subconscious forms within us. They were kept within their original sphere both religiously and socially. In our time this experience and a whole list of other earlier experiences are not available.

Holidays organized the year; the very anticipation of a holiday was meaningful and tended to create order. It can fill us with nostalgia or yearning when we are forced to admit that this kind of spontaneous experience has been lost to us for the time being. But nostalgia will do no good, nor will efforts and studies. Spontaneity cannot be won in this way. But this example makes it easy to see that such losses, if they are not to lead to disease, force man to undertake certain tasks.

The example of holidays can also show us that, when social-communal or religious benefits are lost, then *individual* care and activity must take their place. More and more, the individual has to take responsibility for what was earlier the role of institutions, customs, morals, and norms. In Chapter 6 we will come back to the question of what to do about holidays.

Other thoughts suggest themselves as well. David Oistrach, the great Russian violinist, once said (he may have borrowed the idea from Franz Liszt), "If I don't practice for two days, then I notice it when I perform. If I don't practice for four days, then the critics notice. If I don't practice for a week, the public notices." When he made this statement, he was at the peak of his career. He had already achieved what it was possible for him to achieve, but for him to *stay* at this summit, he had to practice for about five hours a day. We are not great virtuosos, neither with the violin nor (which is more relevant) with regard to our psychological, moral, and cognitive problems. And yet we are silently of the opinion that we can solve these problems just as we are, without even once trying to exercise these faculties: without "practice."

Such a position is not very logical or realistic. For the human being of today it is of great importance to arrive at this insight: we have to do something to become healthy and to remain healthy. It was to support this insight that the previous chapters discussed the general situation in mental health so extensively.

This doing consists, to a large extent, of not doing; that is, certain activities should be allowed to stop while others are taken up into the rhythm of one's life. Most people who have personal difficulties—and this means, necessarily, that they also have problems with other people—don't realize that a part or even the whole of these difficulties arise through their own doing. We will have many opportunities in what follows to discuss moments in which one can gain an *overview of one's mental life*. From such vantage points over one's life, one can review the day, the week, the month, the year, and make an approximate judgment on the harmlessness or harmfulness of one's habits. One may also estimate the lack of balance in one's acquired, everyday forms of behavior. To achieve better health for the soul, the general tendency will be to bring the I-being to a more intense self-experience. This strengthened I-being can then receive the mental and spiritual energies now trapped by subconscious habits. Habits themselves—but without power over the autonomous soul—will then serve as the ground, the loam, in which a spiritual life can grow to fruition.

If the self-experience of the soul were as intense as an experience of physical touch, then most people would have no mental problems. They would know that they *are* without need of proofs and confirmations (which can, in any case, only be valid for a subject that already *is*). Uncertainty on this point is egotism, and it brings with it all of life's problems. We have seen that man has the possibility, today, to experience himself in living presentness. To do so would constitute the universal cure to problems of the soul, that is, to grasp present consciousness by means of developing one's awareness. It has also been shown that this is a great *task* that man must assume himself: it will not come to him on its own. When experience of the *I* is possible but not actual, it leads to a restriction of consciousness to its own past and this makes up the common grounds for the disease. We must take as our goal the elimination of these causes of disease. Individual symptoms can only be dealt with alongside this central goal.

The strategy for a better health of the soul can be thought of in the following way as it applies to subconscious forms of sensation and of will. Such forms are monsters, whether large or small, whose size and power stem from energies taken away from the *I*. Have you ever looked at a spider or a mosquito through a magnifying glass? A mere tenfold enlargement, and they look like dangerous mythical beasts. Imagine one the size of an elephant. Confronted with a spider or a mosquito of this size, you would certainly not try to fight it unarmed, and you have no internal weapons. But these creatures have gained their tremendous size with energies stolen from you. If you can win back these energies, your own life blood, then these beings will shrivel up like swollen balloons as the air leaks out. Something similar happens when autonomous I-energies are exercised. The alienated energy forms are sapped of their strength and the energies are returned to their rightful master. The monsters shrink until they are no longer a threat, and there is no need to worry about them: they collapse.

Today's human being is *driven* and *pushed* by life, by the everyday things around him, by inner habits and by resonance, for the whole of his waking hours. In ancient Greece secluded holy areas, *Temenoi,* were intended to create a region protected from the rush of everyday life in which man could be alone with his gods. These protected spatial regions, cut off from all profanity and saved for the purely divine and human, find their contemporary equivalent today in intervals of time, oases in time, during which one does something that is neither necessary for his everyday life nor a result of subconscious impulses, but which is rather a purely autonomous decision and activates the energies of the *I*. At the beginning it does not matter what specific thing we do. These ten to twenty minutes, repeated every day, form a "place" in which the autonomous essence of man can become stronger. Free energies can order themselves, structure themselves, in this place. And in cases where it is not possible for someone to be autonomously active for ten minutes without falling into associations, the presence of another person, the aid of a friend or therapist, can help. In this case it is particularly helpful for the relevant person to report in words on what took place during those ten minutes.

The time oasis establishes a base for the mental health measures to be undertaken by contemporary man. In what follows we will consider how such an oasis can be used and what other measures may be added to it. These measures must do justice to man's double nature: he lives in the world together with other people; he also has his private life as an individual.

Speaking and Listening

All through life, we are called upon to speak. One's relationship with oneself and with others occurs through words, and words then call up mental pictures and will impulses. Most of mankind feels an urge to say more than is strictly necessary. This unnecessary speaking is not always on a different level of discourse from necessary speech. What level is that, after all?

It is the level of *information*. This refers to all those times when we say something that has already been thought, as opposed to something new, something never before communicated, something freshly thought at that moment. And this *must* take place; we have to inform others and receive information from them. This kind of speech serves everyday life. There is nothing to object to here, we only note that it is not the only possibility; words can have other functions as well.

But not all communicated information is equally important from the standpoint of practical life. There is plenty of superfluous information, gossip, and chatter. Why does this exist at all? As we described in Section 3.4, gossip always carries an egotistical satisfaction by concerning itself with the weaknesses, failings, and failures of other people. But the other important thing to realize about this is that it nevertheless shows, albeit in a low, twisted form, the activity of a fundamental impulse to speak. This impulse is itself *true speech:* man uses speech to make his humanity real rather than potential; he exercises the reality of his existence as man. Speaking in terms of feelings, we could say that people long for the warmth of conversation. Naturally, gossip gives them no access to this warmth, no more than drinking satis-

97

fies a passion for liquor: it only increases the desire to drink. Because gossip never satisfies the longing for the warmth of the word, for understanding and being understood by others (on the contrary, it promotes the colder element of antipathy), unright speech perpetuates itself as an alcoholic perpetuates his own drinking.

In Goethe's fairy tale about the green snake and the white lily, there is a remarkable conversation. The golden king asks questions and the snake answers:

What is finer than gold?
Light.
What is quicker than light?
Conversation.

Quicker here (German: *erquicklich*) is meant in the old sense of alive or refreshing. Yet few conversations could be called refreshing. What would such conversations be like?

Certainly, there should be nothing "finished" in such a conversation, nothing that has already been thought and spoken many times before. And what someone says should not be listened to as if its contents were already known; it should not be heard beneath the echo of counterarguments and the shadow of the coming answer. Rather, one should meet the speech of others with the greatest possible inner stillness, a receptive silence. And this will influence the speaker, too. He will be ashamed to say anything unmeaningful or to use old forms of thought and speech. This silence with which speech should be met should be like the attentive listening of a child as the child learns to speak. The child *wants* to know and cannot put up an ego against what he hears, because as yet he has no ego. *Right speech* begins with right listening, which prepares us to understand others. This kind of understanding, which can never be substantiated by words or outer signs, is directed not only toward what is said, but toward the other human being who speaks. When the other person speaks from his presentness, from what is now going on inside him, from what he is just now experiencing, instead of from a set routine, then the word can blossom between two people. Even what was already known earlier can be experienced *newly* for this kind of conversation. Every teacher knows the difference between the effect of a lecture given from memory and a lecture during which what is said is now said anew, newly thought, newly understood.

The warmth, the refreshment, the nourishment of conversation lies between the words, above the words—in the *word* —in understanding. Most refreshing of all is the completely wordless understanding—in the *word*—that rarely, in lucky moments, lights up between people. A conversation always happens between two people, even when it seems that many are speaking to one another or one is addressing many: it is always one to one.

In such an ideal conversation the essence and the wonder of language, even of wordless language, reveals itself: its sacredness, which makes possible the miracle of a bridge between two separated consciousnesses. It seems as if, with the closing of the fontanel, man shut himself off in consciousness from everyone else. Yet a far-reaching communion and communication is nevertheless possible, without the aid of any physical, mechanical, or biological connection. These latter tend to exclude linguistic or spiritual connectedness, because such connectedness is not an effect; it depends on nothing that has not gone through a process of understanding.

Language really exists so that man can exercise and realize his humanity through it. Without speaking, a human is not really human, and this means that without an interlocutor a human is not really human. In earlier times this partner in conversation was the godhead—his first "thou"—and today it is the nearest godhead: his neighbor, another human being.

Man has gone through much
and named many of the Divine
since we have become a conversation
and can hear of one another

99

This is how Hölderlin speaks about men and gods. But the miracle that

> *we are a conversation*
> *and hear of one another*

applies to men among themselves as well.

We saw in Section 1.3 how linguistic ability comes about in man divinely or superconsciously, and accompanies us as a superconscious ability throughout life. This holy faculty, belonging to the innermost essence of man, is active on an unworthy plane when it serves as a currency for the exchange of information, even if this is taken as a matter of course today. Nearly all the myths and popular traditions on earth tell of the heavenly, divine origin of language (also of reading and writing). To talk nonsense—speaking to kill time or to say something worthless—is just as unnatural, from this perspective, as speaking in order to lie, in order to hide one's own intentions, or in order to mislead others. Man causes most of the evil in the world, even when it hurts his human dignity, by means of language. It is a deep truth that when language is decadent, mankind is in danger.

It should come as no surprise, then, that *right speech* is seen as one of the fundamental measures in the health of the soul. Unright speech mostly harms the person who uses it, not his interlocutor. He uses, or rather misuses, the most luminous superconscious faculty by applying it in a distorted, spoiled fashion to an inappropriate plane. If man misuses his speaking, the most essential higher faculty, how can his mental life go smoothly? Speaking is our means of achieving a clear understanding with others; inner speech is part of this as well. "That which cometh out of the mouth, this defileth a man." (Matthew 15:11) "But those things which proceed out of the mouth come forth from the heart; and they defile the man. For out of the heart proceed evil thoughts . . . ." (Matthew 15:18,19) And the kinds of evil thoughts are then listed.

Because language happens in *life,* as the most common

activity, the most common measure in mental hygiene should be practiced in *life*, in the everyday world: right speech. It cannot be practiced alone. It can be practiced during the time oases or, if possible, outside of these times. Every day, or every day on which one intends to do the exercise, one must determine in advance a moment during which one will have a conversation with another person. The exercise consists in several phases, which can be practiced separately or together. In the beginning, it may be advisable to practice a different phase each time; later they can be combined to form a complete exercise.

The first phase of the exercise is right listening, which we could also call *right silence*. One tries to perceive the other person, that is, the *speaker* in him, not his outer appearance. This requires the most thorough attentiveness possible. At first, one must be attentive in *thought:* that is, one tries not to think one's own thoughts, which rise up during the discourse of the other person by way of response, criticism, supplemental observation, or agreement, but rather one makes an effort to think in step with the other, the speaker's, thoughts. From time to time one considers whether one has really understood the other's words, or whether contradictions have not come up through misunderstanding. The next step is then to try to be attentive with deeper levels of the soul, to perceive the speaker with one's feeling. This requires total silence on the part of all sympathy and antipathy, even when spontaneous; it is not a question of the feelings that the speaker calls up *in me,* but of a purely cognitive *feeling,* by which I feel *him,* just as a work of art or a landscape can be experienced through its own feeling hue.

In this inner silence all agreement or disagreement, criticism or pleasure, regarding the *content* of what is said, must be put to rest. For example, judgment should arise in us about the quality of what has been said. Judgments and answers will be more forthright and faster, the more we are *awake* while *listening,* that is to say, absorbed in the speaker and not distracted by our own thoughts and an immediate critical reaction.

It is clear that this small, harmless exercise of right listening or right silence is not at all simple; it requires and presupposes a whole suite of inner gestures. Particularly if we take into account that the absorption we have talked of must be neither a pose nor a cramped, strained attitude. It may be unavoidable for it to begin as a pose, but gradually one can work at the realization of this gesture so as to dissolve the pose and replace it with real interest: it is a pose as long as one does not know *what is to be done*. And straining does appear, at the beginning, in every exercise, and can even be felt as a bodily cramping. The dissolution of such cramps is an exercise in itself. A cramped exercise is no exercise, just as one cannot be artistically active when cramped. This dissolution is not sufficient if it goes no further than a loosening of bodily cramps. If the mental cramp is not taken care of, the physical tightness will soon reappear. Mental straining can best be dissolved by imagining natural processes that are completely cramp free and then trying to live into and become one with these processes. Appropriate pictures for this exercise could be the way a leaf moves in the wind—not taken away by the wind, remaining on its twig, but lightly, with no resistance. Or the way a swan lightly, effortlessly floats on the water, the way a cloud sails in the sky; the way a leaf bends under the weight of the snow until finally the snow slides smoothly off. But it is best for you to find your own examples. During this exercise it is particularly useful not to gratify the frequently felt impulse to interrupt and interject some comment while the other person is speaking, but still to notice that the impulse is there. Slowly the impulse itself will disappear. Such renunciation stimulates the power of the autonomous I-being.

In time, this conversational silence will grow from being a negative, renouncing gesture to a positive, helpful mental attitude. Our inner stillness not only counterbalances most disturbances and difficulties, it also builds a friendly dwelling place for the other person's words, a presentiment that he will be understood. And he or she will have an easier time speaking, and speaking well. This receptivity is just as little an agreement as a disagreement with the content of what is said. One's understanding must be free of all judgment and may even help the speaker to understand himself or herself properly.

You will notice that this exercise, like the following exercises, works counter to habits and to the impulses of the subconscious. Everything consciously, intentionally undertaken by the autonomous I-being goes against the current of subconsciously motivated habits. This is one of the reasons why the exercises generally should not and cannot be extended over the whole day. They are to be limited to a planned time span of ten to thirty minutes. They will work their way more strongly into the whole course of our day the less we worry about them outside of the assigned time of the exercise. When the time for the exercise is over, life should be lived spontaneously and without concern. Of course this does not mean that one pays no attention to language. For example, one should not listen to the unright speech of others if this is not necessary; one should not listen in, therefore, if one has nothing to do with the conversation. Unright speech is always woven with unright feelings, which attract us and cause unhealthy attitudes of the soul in the listeners. When he wanders through hell, Dante listens eagerly to the virtuoso argument between two of the damned so that his guide, Vergil, first scolds and then comforts him.

And merely think, that I am always by you
If it ever happens that chance leads you
Where people argue so,
For it is a low desire to hear such things.

When right hearing has been practiced for some time and has taught us something, then the exercise can be taken further by means of another not doing. One tries to make sure not to say anything superfluous, not to speak just to have something to say, not to gossip. Naturally, it is difficult to determine what is superfluous, and conversations can be investigated in this light after they are over. We are often

tempted to say something that we could very well leave unsaid. When this renunciation is realized, it will be noticed
that forces flow from us that make possible a better understanding of what was left unsaid. By renouncing gossip, energies trapped in the subconscious come under the direction of
the speaking I-being. One should particularly be aware of
impulses to speak ill of a third party, to discuss their failings,
which one would never do if they were present. It is useful to
ask oneself, would I say that to him or her directly? And one
simply does not say anything that one would not say in front
of the person involved. One should also renounce saying
anything in the absence of the person that one could say in
his or her presence.

Naturally these suggestions do not represent fixed rules.
There are cases when one must interrupt the speaker. It is to
be done gently, without emotion and without stirring up his
or her emotions. There are cases when one has to speak of
someone who is not present, but this should be done as far
as possible as if the person *were* present.

When the more passive aspects have been practiced—listening and renunciation of superfluous speaking—then the
more positive parts of the exercise can be addressed. This
part is easily formulated: one says something only when one
has something to say. You may have the impression that even
this part of the exercise would consist of silence!

How often, in fact, do we really have something to say to
our fellow beings? There is a real truth here. We have seen
that the adult rarely thinks a new thought. But in right speech
it is not a question of new thoughts, or of the content of
what is spoken at all. Speaking is always speaking to and
with someone, so that the content and the manner is determined by the partner with whom we are speaking. And so
the content of the conversation is not the whole of it, for
example when the emphasis is on speaking *to* someone in
order to bring him or her into the conversation or in order
to comfort the other person so that he or she will feel part of
human society. Naturally, all this can also take place in silence, suggested simply by one's behavior; this often works
even better than words. Right speech does not mean that one

gives forth only pearls of wisdom: this speech must be right for the situation. "I have something to tell you"—and the "something" and the "you" form a unity, neither of which can be right by itself. Often this something is hard or impossible to express: the formulation of such things should not be given up quickly, but if it is impossible, then a wordless speaking can very well occur, and it is often a better kind of speech.

We always speak to someone. It is worthwhile to think this thought through. What we say should therefore always be individual, according to our partner in conversation. A lecturer has the same problem, only in a more complicated form, because he or she often has to take a diverse public into account. If a lecture is at all good then it is a conversation: the lecturer has to feel what is right, and when it is right for the listeners. He or she has to *hear* how they stand in relation to what is said and be concerned with a great deal that flows from the audience.

Economy with words has nothing to do with a pose of frugality: too little is no better than too much. Speak in such a way that the partner is *stimulated to understand*. Speak in such a way that your partner is stimulated to think further may be a better formulation.

Conversation is always a source of the unexpected, of the improvised, and the more it is, the better the conversation, for it always leads to surprises. Thus conversation is a continuing exercise of spiritual presence in words. Many people have problems with just this quality; the "right" answer doesn't occur to them immediately, but comes up often much later, after the conversation is over. If we ask why this happened, and if we call to mind our mood and our gestures at the time, we can ascertain that we were not being matter of fact. Our attention was divided between the matter at hand and, perhaps, the will to be successful in the conversation, to do it right, to assert ourselves, and so on. The exercise that works on concentrated awareness can help us to say the right thing at the right time, as we will see in the course of this chapter.

The unexpected may also come up in unsuccessful conversations, but here it will have the quality of a destructive force. These are always cases in which the personal is addressed; instead of an ideal content, the words seek to bring about personal feelings or to mobilize personal feelings toward some end. This introduces an element that is actually quite foreign to conversation. It does not belong to the word, and it chases after a goal that lies outside of the conversation. Because it speaks to the personal, generally egotistical element within us, it is naturally difficult to respond rightly, that is, in accord with the original purpose of the conversation. On the other hand, it is very easy to meet this attempt at disrupting us from out of our own egotistical side. The difficulty of the right answer lies here in the fact that we are distracted from a matter-of-fact attentiveness and led away into the personal realm. The best method, when we discover an attempt to distract us (and we do not always discover it, in which case the attempt is successful) is to leave a pause before answering. This brings the disruptive speaker out of his rhythm and gives us the chance to drop personal considerations and give an answer that is really to the point, while taking the attempt to distract us into full consideration.

When I have said something and then receive the answer, I should again be listening with an inner stillness. I also pay attention to whether and how much I have been understood by my partner. It may well be that he or she has understood my thoughts better, more deeply, than I did myself. This is the case when I am not practiced in expressing myself or when my partner in conversation knows the subject matter, or me, particularly well.

Let it be emphasized once more that right speech is an exercise and so it should be tried out in a limited, predetermined time span, not spread out over the entire day. Its intensity would almost certainly be insufficient for this. A short but intensive exercise will gradually have an effect on the whole day. It is clear that this exercise, like all the others, can be deepened infinitely, since, in order to speak rightly, I must know the truth; in order to speak rightly, I must know my partner. But how far, how deeply, do I know the truth and the human with whom I am speaking? This task is unending.

The apostle James in his letter (3:2) says, with good reason: "For in many things we offend all. If any man offend not in word, the same is a perfect man, and able also to bridle the whole body."

The whole of a human life could be right speech: this is a distant, nearly unreachable goal. But if we do not strive for the unattainable, we will not achieve the attainable either.

How to Deal with Time

It must have become clear to the reader by this time that the human being today has to do something for his mental health. This something and this doing are certainly limited, in terms of both time and intensity; we can't spend the whole day worrying about our souls. This would be just as wrong as doing nothing and it would take us away from our tasks and duties in life. At the start, this doing should be limited to a minimum—we all have so little time! Our grandparents had far, far less comfort, fewer labor-saving machines—did they have less time? We have two work-free days in the course of the week, and we work shorter hours. How is it that we still have no time? Where does the saved-up time go to? Is the writer Michael Ende right after all in his book *Momo* when he says that someone has stolen our time? It is not a bad idea to give an account of what you do with your time. Such an account would show that we are not very economical with this resource. But to learn to use time more effectively, we have to live more consciously. This means that we should not give ourselves over to *any* spontaneity in this matter, just as we learned to use our legs when we learned to walk or our hands when we learned to grasp and point, or our speech organs when we learned to speak. *Everything* is instinctive for an animal: a baby tiger, separated from birth from its kind and released as an adult into the wild, can do practically everything necessary for its life, for communications, for mating, and so on. Man must be protected, taken care of, before he can survive and maintain himself independently in life. This can last twenty, sometimes thirty or fifty years long.

This individual need to learn, to do things consciously, extends with time to new areas, which in earlier epochs were managed by social institutions. It is the same with the division of time. There is a need for times when man can review his lifestyle, judge it, set goals, notice changes. These times could be called "lookouts," which we can visit every year, every half year, during holidays, or every month. A little looking foward and back, evaluation, planning, questions and answers: this is the content of the lookout. This is how we begin to shape our time: we decide on a mental health measure or decide to switch from one measure to another. The only exercise to be recommended at all times is, as we pointed out in Section 4.2, the exercise of right speech.

Man may be in need of many such measures, but to begin with he can only take on a few, in part because of his lack of time. By way of comfort let me say that the effort to do away with *one* bad habit, for instance, unright or superfluous speech, gradually wears away *all* habits, has an effect on them all, even those with which the practiced exercise seems to have nothing in common.

Gradually, the practicing human makes a discovery. The exercise (fifteen minutes of right speech, for instance, every day or every two days) is something unpleasant at first, an added difficulty in a life that was hard enough beforehand. But after some time one notices that the unpleasantness disappears and the moment comes when the exercise offers greater and greater joy for us; a good kind of joy, not only and not principally concerned with success, but similar to the joy of artistic activity, the joy of doing. After reaching a certain level of proficiency, in art as in the health of the soul, contentment and joy will follow. This is in fact the way to tell whether or not the practice is working properly. The amount of time necessary for this will be quite different from person to person. As experience shows, it is not a question of an egotistical joy, and part of the exercise consists in just this, that we learn to distinguish between an egotistical, self-feeling joy and *pure* joy.

When a certain satisfaction takes place during the exercise a second exercise can be attempted. One *can* take up two exercises at the very start, depending on time, on strength, and on insight. Which one to choose second depends more or less on the following considerations.

Once a person wakes up from his dreamlike absorption in the day, then he begins to ask questions: What is our time for? Or what is the purpose of life? These are questions that cannot be answered from outside, by another human being, because every answer would have to be understood and judged, perhaps agreed to, by my own activity. But one thing can be said: perhaps *one* meaning lies in following up such vast questions, thinking about them, trying to learn and find and cognize what is necessary for answering these questions. It may happen that just when the question comes up we are engaged in something else, in life, in responsibilities, in relationships. In such a case, we have to forgo thinking about such questions for a long time at a stretch, but it is still important to learn to live with these questions, even in their unsolved state.

Once we begin to live consciously with these questions, once we have consciously given our life some direction, then the question about the purpose of life can in fact be answered succinctly. Only in this way can human beings be responsible for their lives, responsible to themselves and to others. Once we have set ourselves a goal, we can then test to see whether we are dealing with time appropriately for the purpose of this goal.

But we should say now, very clearly, that if one sets oneself a goal out of egotistical motives, then no exercise, no measures, will help. More precisely: it is not merely that, for practical reasons, such goals will not be helped, but also I intend to provide *no support for egotistical goals*. The practical reasons for this are found in Section 3.3. The principle of egoism leads, quite obviously as has been shown, to the war of all against all. I refuse to contribute to such a process. To aid such goals is one of the greatest crimes against mankind. Yet still, tricks and techniques for completely egotistic goals are widely sold: for success in your business life, in your love life, in society, and so on. Just read the ads in the local paper. In this book the intention is to help *human beings,* not the enemy of the human that lives within us. Egotism is the central disease of mankind, and every technique recommended here serves in one way or another to conquer egotism and to promote the experience of the *I* instead of the experience of the ego. Egotism prevents adults from giving themselves as devotedly to their listening in conversation as children do when they learn to speak. Because every technique and every exercise is always an exercise in concentrated attention, every exercise taken up out of egotism will fail.

One widespread human weakness consists in not being able to summon one's powers of thought, so that, for example, one finds it difficult to say the right thing at the right time in conversation. The therapeutic technique here is to try to stay with one theme in thought, when there is time, for example at the train station, in the dentist's office, or in a train, as opposed to giving oneself up to associations and having all kinds of vivid images pass through consciousness, with the predominance of one's current concerns. The chosen theme should not be something important. The less it concerns me personally, the more suited it is to develop the "muscle power" of concentration. As you may imagine, this exercise will never succeed if undertaken for egotistical motives as, for example, in order to *be successful* in conversation instead of in order to better represent the truth. Such egotistical motives always distract the attention. And one cannot say, in such cases, "I won't think about it!" Just try for five minutes not to think about a green elephant.

Of course the "truth" is often *our* truth. That is, apart from its objective truth value we are often *personally* interested in the discussion, for example, through ambition. It is difficult to discover this personal dimension within *our* interest in the truth. One of the first tasks is to cultivate just this ability to distinguish clearly. Egotism can come up in a thousand guises; the greatest of wise men is not safe from it.

If one tries to organize one's soul with an orientation to

health, that is, to form it consciously, then one thing is of
great importance. All exercises seek to dismantle the *finished
human being*, habits and well-worn tracks of the life of the
soul, and to call into life an *unfinished* human being capable
of improvisation, assigning him his legitimate role. Briefly
stated: one seeks to dissolve certain aspects of oneself and to
form a real subject, that is, to bring oneself to self-experience
instead of self-feeling. These two efforts should be made in
balanced fashion, because habits are temporary supports that
man needs if his true subject, the *I*, is not strong enough to
always take the reins in hand by itself. On the other hand,
exercises to strengthen the *I* cannot succeed if habits are too
strong. In that case exercises aimed at concentrating the attention would only make the habitual man stronger. This is
why exercises and techniques must always be directed in both
directions. Right speech corresponds to both objectives at
once. The concentration exercise described here strengthens
the I-being. One can ask oneself in the lookouts: what is
happening in me, in my soul, without my will, without my
accord? What is happening in such a way that it remains,
perhaps must remain, opaque for me? A prejudice for or
against something, which comes straight out of feeling with
no grounding in thought, is an example of the habitual,
which is to be carefully dissolved.

If one is unsuccessful in gathering one's thoughts around a
single, predetermined, indifferent theme, then it is good to
first concentrate and focus one's attention on the process of
perception. As the object of an exercise in concentration one
always chooses a natural object, such as a stone or crystal, a
landscape, a tree or plant, a sky with clouds, or the voices
and tones of nature. The exercise consists in observing exactly what is there. Normally one is content with defining the
object, rather than with really perceiving it. One could not
picture it for oneself realistically, but only as a stock item, a
robot version of itself. After all, we all know how a rose, a
tree, a cloud looks. We should be aware that nothing in
nature repeats itself; no rose exactly resembles another; no
cloud exactly resembles another cloud nor even itself, be-

cause it changes with time and varied lighting. Only these unique views are what we mean by perception in the exercise. We can perceive a great deal that absolutely cannot be described with words and concepts—colors, forms, movements, tones—yet we can certainly see, hear, touch, or smell these details. In the exercise one pays attention to just these inexpressible details that cannot be concretely thought, but can be very closely followed by perception. Perception proceeds conceptually even when *formulated* concepts for what has been perceived are lacking. In perception, we can make unbelievably minute distinctions, without being able to express them.

The perception exercise is easier for many people than the gathering of thoughts, and can therefore be undertaken as a first step toward concentration of thought. We can consider how much perception gives to us in our childhood, how full the individual perceptions are then in comparison with those of an adult, and how for a child *everything* in the perceptual world is interesting. The adult passes over everything that doesn't immediately concern him. The mysterious, continually new world of the child becomes well-known and boring scenery in the adult's everyday life. Perceptions are alive, and qualitatively of a quite different kind for children than they are for adults. This exercise brings back something of what has been lost.

Within oneself one finds distracting factors in the life of the soul, moods and states of mind that often appear justified and caused by external conditions. These moods, however, are often only *apparently* justified, and generally, outer circumstances or events are only a pretext for states of mind that grow from deep roots within us. As is well known, many *fears* do not go away when all external grounds have been removed. Generally, people look around for external reasons for their moods and states of mind. And these can always be found: moods, when they make themselves felt, are always negative, and there are always reasons in this world for negative feelings. A typical figure is the otherwise well-tempered boss who sometimes gets up on the wrong side of bed: then the office is rife with failures, incompetences, trouble. Naturally, people suffer from their moods, but they also enjoy negative feelings. For many people their daily anger, combined with a disdain for the people who "caused" it, is just as important as their daily bread.

If moods are carried outward, that is, if a reason for them is projected outward, then further negative waves of feeling arise among the people who come into contact with them. The effect returns on the one who began it, and a continually increasing resonance of such feelings takes place. Therefore it is therapeutic as far as possible not to turn negative feelings outward either in order to "enjoy" negative feelings or in order to develop so-called pity. The renunciation of any external living out of these feelings, if undertaken consciously, is a first step, but the way in which it is done is more important than the fact alone.

A person can put on a mask, masquerading that he feels well, that he is a good person. Everything depends on how *completely* this is done, how undivided is the soul's gesture. If in spite of mental pain or inner bitterness, we can still take part in the problems of others and comfort them or give advice with goodwill, then *this* mask works beneficially on one's own suffering. The less the mask is participated in, then the more unreal it is, up to the point of being actually harmful, so that in that case it would really be better to let loose the anger than to have negative feelings ferment and increase beneath a cold mask. From one's own pain one can learn sensitivity for the life of one's neighbor; from one's own pain one can also become unmerciful toward others. Anger and hate are the feelings most difficult to control. They are also the ones most easily projected outward.

Renunciation of superfluous speech brings cognitive energies to the I-being. Renunciation of *immediate* verbal response, and of the inner formulation of intuitively won knowledge, is also recommended. By holding back verbally, the living elements are preserved from a too early decay and distortion through speech, although this latter is nearly unavoidable. Only poets and gifted writers can put something living into language without distortion. Normally our formulations in language exhibit our conformity to habitual ideas and turns of phrase and to half-conscious pictures.

Normal feelings, even negative ones like hate and anger, are alive. This is why they have such power over consciousness. It is only when we express these feelings through acts or through formulation in language that they take on form, and we recognize them as hate for someone or fear of something. Unexpressed, they remain alive and therefore capable of being transformed. If we abstain from living them out, something happens analogous to when we sustain fresh insights and knowledge without expressing them. What works against this is the impulse to enjoy negative feelings the way we enjoy negative gossip about absent persons. Therefore this kind of renunciation, of forbearance, is difficult, and its value depends to a great extent on how it is done.

Take two extreme cases. First take someone who represses his or her anger or bad mood, and puts on an indifferent or benevolent mask—an empty mask. Everyone will feel this mask to be an empty form. None of the negative feelings find their way to daylight, but they boil within the person all the more. This has little therapeutic value. The second case would be someone who disappears into the mask completely, and thereby the mask is soon no longer a mask at all: then the still-living negative feelings transform themselves into I-energies. And the person wins for himself or herself a standpoint from which to look back on the bad mood, the anger, the hate: and they reveal themselves, without their former power.

The secret of this second case is that the person has to do something. This also lies behind the healthy distracting effect of new, difficult tasks for someone recently bereaved. Generally, success comes with something that lies between the two extreme cases. To repress the negative waves of feeling does little or no good; to find and take up tasks with interest and energy can substantially reduce the power of moods and states of mind. This is also the secret of good or bad imitation. We can imitate a model from the outside, or we can imitate a model by grasping it in the innermost kernel of our being, as a child does or as Zen students try to do when imitating the master. It is clear from the foregoing that every attempt to step out of one's habitual role and step into another role has a therapeutic effect.

One of the most common weaknesses is a weak will. How often we know what is to be done, yet do nothing! To conquer or at least partially correct this failing, there is a very easy exercise: to do nothing, that is, to *intentionally* do nothing. One sets the intention to do nothing on the following day, at a particular time, for from one to five minutes. How do you do nothing? You stand or sit or walk back and forth and think, "These minutes are set aside for me to withdraw from all activity. The only thing I'll do is to think of a completely superfluous activity that has no practical purpose, no meaning, that I *could* carry out from my will alone." Such an activity would be, for example, to untie and then tie up again either my necktie or my shoelaces. Or to draw a geometrical figure like a pentagon on a piece of paper and then pace it out in the room, or to walk in a circle in a particular direction. I imagine this activity. Then, I decide whether I am going to carry it out or not. If I decide to carry it out, then I do so. If I decide not to carry it out, then I imagine it in as much detail as possible. The essential thing here is that the activity should not be anything *useful*. In this way one progresses from nondoing, perhaps, to the imagination of a superfluous activity, and from this imagination, perhaps, to the execution of the useless activity. This exercise strengthens the *I*.

A further general principle for this technique is that one should divide everything into the *smallest possible steps*, and then perform these steps. This is particularly helpful when an exercise is too difficult in its entirety and does not succeed. And this principle applies to the exercises as a whole: one should not take up too many at once.

In the little technique to strengthen the will, fantasy plays a part, and this is important. One is to think up something superfluous, some useless activity. This activity of the fantasy is itself therapeutic, because today's man, controlled by his form of life, has let his fantasy dry up. This starvation of one's powers of fantasy gets compensated by an excess of perceptions, an addiction to perception, as we see in addiction both to television and to low-quality literature. As already mentioned, a substitute never satisfies these needs, and so the unsatisfied person needs ever more intensive and more varied kinds of substitutes. The greatest fantasy novels, such as the *Lord of the Rings* by Tolkein or the *Never-Ending Story* by Michael Ende, owe their popularity in part to the fact that they lead the reader into a world of good fantasy (Goethe would have called it exact fantasy). Here is no escapism, no flight from an unlovely reality into an unreal loveliness, but a worthy liberation of a neglected human faculty: fantasy. Such is, indeed, the very theme of the *Never-Ending Story*. These and similar artistic pursuits, along with many science fiction novels, have a healing, beneficial effect; but this effect depends to a great extent on *how* they are read. We are referring here above all to the intensity of the imaginative function: such novels, with their unusual imagery have an effect on the reader's fantasy according to how far he or she really places these images in the mind's eye; how far the person uses his or her *own* fantasy. This example lets us judge clearly how much more activity is required for reading than for listening to the radio; how much more for listening to the radio than for watching television. This is also one of the most important differences between the theater and film. In film much can be *shown* that, in theater, theatergoers have to *do* by themselves. Of course the technique of letting much go unsaid, unshown, in film, can have the same artistic effect; but this is done only rarely.

As an exercise, fantasy can also be put into practice by itself. We should not fall into *associative fantasy,* to which we are very prone: we fantasize half-consciously when we "have time" for it. These moments can be used for little exercises like the concentration of thought on one theme. One such exercise would be a fantasy exercise. In associative fantasy, we are led by desires, ideas of pleasure, or else by images of painful situations, images of sorrow, or of our own failures. Each of these pictures is ruled and guided by the feeling life. A willed fantasy should replace this subconsciously driven association. The most varied themes will do here: the exact imagination of a landscape, of a tree, of a bird, of the cloudy sky; or else one can imagine a never before seen landscape, garden, or tree. It need not be a scene without movement; one may very well introduce movement through wind, through changes of lighting. It can be a scene with people, known or unknown. But one thing is essential: it should be neither pleasant nor unpleasant, but rather matter-of-fact, exact, not superficial. If this representation in pictures goes well, then one may also try to capture the pictures expressively, in words.

For all these exercises and techniques one needs time. Not *much* time, much less in fact than we waste every day. But the fact that we separate out a certain span of time from the day does not mean that we should *hurry* during this time period. On the contrary, this little span of time is more effective the more slowly we go through the exercises and measures we have planned on. This slowness stands in contrast to the habits of modern men, so that it can be taken up as a measure, as an exercise, in itself, and must often be learned.* For the fantasy exercise, we should imagine a naturally slow process: the passage of clouds, the circling of an eagle, a sunrise. In gathering thoughts, the thinking of the theme should go on without haste. The slower we think, the more intensive the thought. Quick thinking is to be practiced by means of slow thinking, just as fast, sure music playing is practiced by slow playing. Every technique for the health of the soul, every exercise, presupposes slow activity.

But there are people who, in their daily activity, are naturally slow, to a painful extent. There are housewives, for example, who cook and clean all day. The result does not, however, correspond to the expenditure of time and energy: another person does everything quickly, and still the apartment is sparkling, the food is delicious. The difference lies in the varied intensity of involvement or concentration. This

* See G. Kühlewind, *Die Diener des Logos*, Chapter V, Stuttgart, 1981.

last can be learned by slowness, but the slowness must go on in full awareness, not while dreaming and fantasizing about other things. It must be slowness that proceeds neither from laziness nor from distraction, but from heightened activity. Slowness can in particular be practiced when eating or drinking, by concentrating the attention on the taste, texture, and smell of the food or drink. One may also exercise this way only on the first few bites and then eat on spontaneously.

Imitation from within, every game in which one transforms oneself and plays a role, is healthy for the soul, brings the soul out of its usual track, and strengthens its freedom and adaptability. In fantasizing, it is healing to imagine living an altogether new role, if possible a nonhuman role, or, if human, then neither sympathetic nor antipathetic: simply foreign, unusual. From this foreign standpoint, that of a fish or a lizard, we try to observe events, situations, stories, without allowing our own interests, feelings, sympathies, to interfere. The hero of a novel may also play out his role before our inner vision, but it should be an exceptional personality, not a type or bit character from a cops-and-robbers story, and we must properly attend to this character.

If we observe the movements of feeling in a normal consciousness, we notice right away that they all have a passive subject, or rather, the subject, man himself, becomes their object; he suffers them. He cannot call them up and, once they are there, he cannot make them stop. It was from this that we concluded that in feeling we are not capable of improvising, as we do in thinking when it really is thinking. Feelings force man into a certain passivity: it is only then that they are really present. Therefore, *doing* something against these feelings is practically the only possibility we have to weaken or overcome them. They overwhelm man: fear, sadness, hate, envy, greed, ambition, bitterness. Egotistical pleasure is also like this, but especially so are the negative feelings that no one wills. All stem from the subconscious. The same could be said of the majority of our habits: they are a form of passivity, like laziness and complacency—we could call them the greatest passions of man—as with a predilection toward superstition and all grasping at dogmas (whether in-

118

stitutional or quite private), the yearning for an authority whom one can recognize and then rely on. Even a quality like greed, which often spurs us to great activity, is suffered passively as a feeling: as far as the *I* goes, no one wants to be greedy.

The passivity of modern man in the face of feeling represents a state of mind that is anachronistic today, although in former times, when the language of the world could still be heard by man, it was the only correct attitude. Then, the less man himself spoke up, the more clearly and completely man was spoken to. With the rise of egotism or past consciousness, passivity becomes the doorway for subconscious impulses in human behavior. Many of us suffer from passivity when faced with feelings, and these feelings then overwhelm us. The extreme case of actual manic-depressive disease clearly reveals that the alternating periods of depression (the "lows") and euphoria are not conditioned by facts, events, or circumstances, but rather originate in the isolated life of the soul. This applies more or less to "healthy" people as well: we notice alternating moods and mental states in ourselves as well. The first step we can take against them—and, as we have seen, only our own activity will help us out of passivity—is to control the expression, the form of expression, and how we carry these emotions *outward*. We renounce our tendency toward exaggeration—at times, we renounce all speech whatsoever. As our strength and circumstances allow, we attempt to speak only at certain times and occasions; later, the silence can be spread out over the entire day. There are many reasons for this exercise, and it has many purposes. Simply being able to pay attention to the movements of the emotions strengthens the autonomous being within us. Avoidance of emotional expression works against the resonance that aggravates emotions, and also prevents our being torn along by their power. Renunciation of carrying out the emotions awakens energies for cognition or, in other words, transforms feeling energies, at least in part, into what they were originally: cognitive feelings. After some practice in this, we notice that renunciation does not as we might think at first muffle the life of feeling. The opposite is true: sensitivity increases, the life of feeling grows more intense. The hues of feeling gradually change: they become purer, in the sense of greater transparency; little by little, a cognitive feeling grows within us, in the heart of normal feelings. But at the start we can experience that the unwilled, spontaneous expression of a feeling is always exaggerated, suitable only to strengthen the passive suffering of emotions. Renunciation of such expression strengthens experience of sensitivity, not the *power of emotion,* which otherwise takes man unawares.

The exercise of equanimity—equanimity on the outside, controlled intensity of feeling within—has nothing to do with lack of feeling, being blasé, or with an inborn phlegmatic temperament. On the contrary, these things are themselves diseases, to be overcome by exercises and other measures. Equanimity in the good sense means an intensive feeling life, but one which is *experienced* rather than *suffered,* and can be so intense for that very reason. The goal is experience, not suppression of feeling, and not the suppression of *appropriate* expression of feeling. By building up an inner tact, one teaches oneself a capacity for judgment, a capacity for judging within feeling itself (not only within thought), whereby one learns to sense what appropriate expression is, and how to carry it out.

The diseased condition of a lack of feeling, when one feels neither pain nor pleasure, generally arises as a reaction to or a defense against strong experiences of feeling, for example at a funeral, when one feels nothing for the dead friend who was so well loved in life. The condition is suffered passively, just like the emotions, and this is suggestive both as to one's character and to a possible cure: one must *do* something, awaken an interest, possibly a spiritual interest, or simply take up an observation of some kind, such as how a seedling or blossom develops, and then record this development in sketches. Another possibility: take a character in a novel and follow his or her development with intense interest; try to understand how this character's personality is related to what happens to the character. These are merely examples of the kind of matter-of-fact activity that can be practiced in such cases. One can also devote oneself to the personality of a scientist, artist, or soldier, and study all that can be known about the person. Or examine a single question thoroughly, for example: what is the origin of the symbol of the snake biting its own tail? The feeling life awakens as the result of developing interest in a completely different direction.

Passivity in the feeling life is no longer appropriate to our times, as many phenomena attest. Besides the case of lack of feeling, there is a more or less clearly recognizable state in which people seek opportunities to live out a particular feeling. The form of the feeling is already there before it has an object, before any perception or mental picture that could have awakened such a feeling. This often happens in love. It is already there, as a desire, before meeting the person to whom the feeling can be transferred. We see from this how impersonal a subconscious impulse is. Surely it would be more appropriate to meet someone, get to know them, and then come to love them. The same applies to anger, hate, fear, even envy: we seek opportunities to live out such feelings. Thinking, our autonomous consciousness, serves the subconscious: a phenomenon that we see all too often. Appropriate measures must be taken against this if man is to remain man.

Another phenomenon is more positive. In certain cases we can influence feeling by means of conscious activity, for example, when someone tries to feel his way into a new artistic style that he does not at first understand, or cannot enjoy. This often succeeds, and a new feeling has arisen through conscious work. Something similar happens to schoolteachers and teachers of special education: they often grow most fond of the difficult children, after having to work with them intensively. This points to our ability, if not to improvise feelings at will, at least to awaken positive feelings. Negative feelings are generally directed to an object consciously only after they were already held in readiness subconsciously, and therefore no change results.

Passivity and complacency lead inevitably to laziness. Joy in activity, in work, has been fundamentally unlearned by modern man. Work has become an unavoidable evil or a heroic deed. Between these two extreme formulations, which ultimately say the same thing, there lies a forgotten gesture: the joy of doing.

We can grow to love what we do only by doing it fully and completely. What we undertake with divided, distracted attention will always be a burden. Today, many careers have become so senseless that the tasks involved cannot be performed with real devotion. In such cases, something must be found outside of the workplace to which one can devote oneself completely.

Just as a teacher can grow fond of the difficult children, just as we can learn to understand art that we do not at first appreciate, so we can teach ourselves to take pleasure and find satisfaction in our own activity, in physical or mental labor. This is one of the most important tasks before modern man. Passive distractions, an excess of passive perception (television!) are to be judged from this standpoint. It is not surprising if many people, particularly the young, think of lack of will or weakness of will as their greatest problem. "Where is the will supposed to come from? What would give an impulse to the will?" This is how the question is formulated. It expresses no disease, but is rather a precise diagnosis of an evolutionary phase common to much of contemporary humanity. Today, human will no longer has an external source, if all goes well. When external impulses, bypassing one's own judgment, are active, this indicates the presence of those forces that either stem from the subconscious or appeal to it.

A will impulse cannot be drawn from without. If such impulses were available in stores or public agencies, we would always have to ask, what for? Why would anyone buy or even simply pick up such impulses? To put it positively: today man is the only source of his own will; he develops it entirely on his own. Those who deny the possibility of freedom of will need only look at someone suffering from a lack of will. When man does not *will*, the subconscious impulses and antihuman energies alone are active. What was earlier a built-in, *given* will impulse is, today, our capacity to ask questions. The old superconscious life intuition has collapsed; man no longer knows the meaning of life without having to ask about it. These intuitions have changed into the capacity to ask questions consciously, which is present in every halfway normal human being. A question once posed already conceals half the answer within it: we already know what to ask about. What was once *given* as life's meaning institutionally, through the church, social relationships, tradition, is alive today in our ability to *ask*. Whether the fundamental questions are asked or not is a matter of the individual's freedom. Today, he stands in the stillness, the windless absence, of all external impulses: in this protective situation, he could develop his own seeds of originality that do not follow from anything, since there is to be no more *following*. Understanding this state of affairs is called revolution. The revolution is unsuccessful if the lack of will is not recognized for what it is, or if it is experienced only intellectually, not with the whole mind and soul as a cosmic/human zero-point, making it possible for man to *begin*. The more painfully and deeply this break-up is experienced, the closer man comes to his revolution.

And even choosing to do nothing is a choice. You ask, what then is to be done? This, above all: to *know,* for yourself, what is to be done. No one can tell you. It must be an intuitive cognition, because everyday consciousness cannot grasp the "meaning" of a pebble. We have to *pose* the great questions, in order to pursue them and answer, perhaps, some of the smaller ones. When a great question really begins to burn, it has the power to draw us along the path, following after it. And it could be that this path itself becomes the meaning that creates a new basis for our lives.

Plato's *Dialogues* present us with the unique figure of Socrates. His methods of teaching men, stimulating them to think, consisted in a continual asking of questions. He is the master, the model and precursor of the men who today, in the era of the consciousness-soul, develop questioning as a *general* capacity.

Right questioning, as we can experience it in the Platonic

dialogues, belongs to the exercise of right speech. Questioning is an activity of the *I,* a gesture which can have no other source than the *I.* In our age, when this gesture is becoming generally valid, its opposite also appears in never before experienced intensity: the reliance on something else, someone else, authority, superstition (often in "scientific" clothing), the search for dogmas that one can be "certain of." All this belongs to the cult of passivity and the avoidance of making efforts on one's own. People imagine someone can impart advice on the important questions and so one can spare oneself the effort of decision, choice, responsibility, and cognitive work. Such an attitude forgets that one had to choose the advice giver and then agree with or reject the advice once given, and therefore it is impossible to escape responsibility, or to avoid questions of fate, choice, or mental and spiritual life. For the body it is appropriate to go to a doctor, but this would be a serious error with regard to the soul and the spirit, those regions of our possible freedom, where man, in principle, is autonomous.

If, at a particular moment in life when a decision must be made, a person turns to a soothsayer, seer, astrologist, or graphologist, then this gesture can be translated as meaning, "I am going to an 'information booth,' where they'll tell me who I am and what I want."

This would be to consider oneself a finished product, about which someone standing outside oneself could give an accurate report. When we go to such information booths, we abandon the present, nascent free activity and forget that even this is a decision (our final decision). We are assessing the past, the finished part of the human, more highly than the possible activity of our own cognition, the new improvisation, new intuitions. It is the realm of the half-free, fluttering energies (see Section 3.5) which are strengthened by such an attitude, itself the expression of their influence. It is a contradictory gesture, because it does involve an act of choice, but just this is what goes unnoticed. Thereby we can open ourselves to still other influences, which work on us through these half-free energies.

Naturally, we can always talk things over with others and seek advice from "experts." But one should be conscious that one makes one's own decisions and bears full responsibility. And we can ask ourselves this question: is it easier to decide *whom* to ask for advice, who is really fit to give such advice *(how do I know this?)* than to make a well-thought-out decision for oneself?

Self-Feeling or Self-Cognition?
Problems in Experiencing the I.

The above mentioned information booth, where you can find out about yourself, is on the one hand a symptom of passivity, and on the other hand a sign of insufficient certainty, of insufficient self-confidence about the capacity to solve one's problems alone. We have talked a lot about unreal self-experience, which causes uncertainty and the failure of self-confidence, for which men compensate by self-assertiveness and the search for success. In fact, all mental problems stem from this source. Aldous Huxley makes just this point when he writes: "If I only knew who in fact I am, I should cease to behave as what I think I am; and if I stopped behaving as what I think I am, I should know who I am."

We can notice a self-sealing gesture in this: normally I am *consciously* only the one who acts, who seeks to know. In response we can ask, who is supposed to know whom?

It is possible to realize, as I hope I have shown, that egotism is impractical, quite apart from being inappropriate to human beings. But insight is far from a victory over egotism. After all, egotism did not arise through insight; it is completely irrational, fed by the subconscious. Egotistical consciousness is normal, everyday consciousness, which we have also called past consciousness. Therefore it is a tricky, often a dangerous matter, when this consciousness makes up mental pictures of how it ought to be if egotism is to be overcome. Egotistical mentalities cannot form mental pictures of nonegotistical states, but they can receive *ideas* on this subject, since the capacity for *intuition* can occasionally play into egotistical everyday consciousness untouched by any disturbing side factors, just as on the plane of past consciousness all cognitive functions can operate normally. They function by bringing down certain contents from higher, superconscious planes, without being able to experience these consciously.

Both the subconscious dynamic of finished formations in the soul and the self-feeling style of half-free energies disturb the normal functioning of cognitive forces. This disturbance reverses the hierarchical structure of the soul, of consciousness: the contents and the movements of consciousness no longer orient themselves from above to beneath, from higher to lower, but upside down. Healing consists in the reinstatement of the legitimate structure. Now the soul functions in accord with its healthy organization when cognizing, thinking, and particularly when perceiving. Therefore measures aimed at this reinstatement will consist in concentrated, if possible undisturbed and precise, exercise of the cognitive functions.

The reality of the I-being cannot be experienced in past consciousness. Therefore, the lack of self-certainty is inevitable on this plane of consciousness, as is directly shown in the so-called inferiority complex. Like all self-directed feelings, this too has no external cause, and cannot be cured by experiences of success. It has a *real* cause, which has little or nothing to do with what a person achieves or does not achieve in life. The inner cause is a superconsious judgment of the distinction between what I *could* be and what I *am*, between what I might be and what I have realized. Nearly everyone is far from a realization of his intellectual and spiritual capacities and possibilities. This is the true source of all feelings of inferiority and discontent with oneself. If psychology recommends experiences of success as a cure here, this remains a mere treatment of the symptoms, and as is well known, it will have to be continually repeated. It aims at concealing the real situation of the soul, which is not even suspected. Such concealment comes all too easily to humans, even without psychological counsel. The quest for self-confir-mation can take aggressive forms. It can result in a cult of hate, give rise to schemers, liars, daredevils, or cause patho-logical suspicion. Stage fright also belongs among these symptoms. With each new frustration, each new failure, the deeper discontent comes closer to consciousness. Conditions of fear can have manifold secondary causes; basically, they stem from an uncertainty as to our own existence. No unreal fear disappears when the causes are removed, since the true cause lies in inner uncertainty.

These symptoms can hardly be attacked directly. No one becomes concentrated, earnest, good, or clever, by imagining how it would look to exercise concentrated thinking or per-ception, how it would look to be in earnest, to do good, to let one's wisdom grow by allowing it to face appropriate problems.

Where self-confidence seems to be lacking, there is in fact a problem with *who* should be confident, and confident *in whom*. These two are the same person. So-called successes and achievements will not be of fundamental help, though they may do some temporary good. What is needed is a practical education in real self-experience, in a manner never achieved in everyday consciousness.

Instead of *talking* about self-realization, there must be an education of the one who is to realize himself. Once this person is really present, then he *has* realized himself, quite independently of all external activity, success, or recognition. Whoever takes up self-realization as something that must occur outwardly remains dependent on the judgment of oth-ers: he seems "realized" to the extent he is recognized. This is clearly a mere matter of appearance.

All previously mentioned measures and exercises serve real self-realization in this sense. It is, at the same time, simple self-cognition. This is not achieved by grumbling, by con-sidering one's weaknesses, misdeeds and errors, because the person who could cognize and consider this independently and autonomously isn't yet sufficiently *existent*, is not there enough, has not yet sufficiently distinguished and separated himself or herself from the person he or she is considering. This separation of the autonomously knowing element in man is led up to by the exercises and other measures given above.

Self-knowledge does not mean that something static, which *is,* becomes known—by whom could "I" be known? Self-knowledge is possible when the subject, the human being, becomes a knower, that is, when he or she experiences himself or herself as the knower, not as the known or even as *the* known. This experience can only arise during concentrated cognitive activity or during concentrated inner activity as, for example, in the exercise to be described next. What is decisive here is that the *activity* of the autonomous I-being should become as strong, as strongly experienced, as sense perceptions. Whether this is achieved through an act of cognition or an act of will depends on which of these two activities, in a given case, can be strengthened to the desired intensity. The common path toward health and further development consists in a person's trying to bring the stronger sides of the I-being into self-experience in cognition, as a cognizing being. When this autonomous authority is awakened and strengthened, it can, from its own strength, notice the weaker places in the soul, observe them in their hindering or distracting tendencies, and then eliminate their negative effects through indirect exercises of dissolution.

A further exercise is positivity. This is harder, because it comprises several components. Every day, we are confronted with occurrences, facts, people, and situations that we feel or judge as negative. Often what appeared negative at first reveals itself later as positive. The exercise, really a sensible, practical attitude, consists of two steps or stages. First we try to discover something positive in events, people, or situations. This discovery must be a knowledge. It is not a matter of seeing black as white or explaining bad as good; that would be illusion or self-deceit, not an exercise. The positive is to be cognized, *known:* this is the exercise. If nothing positive can be found at present, as may well happen, then one is to seek out the real possibility of a positive development or outcome. Mere fantasy is to be avoided here: the positive outcome must have *known* sources, conditions, in the present; ungrounded assumptions are not relevant. This reveals the complexity of the exercise: a sharp observation and equally sharp faculty of making distinctions are needed to tell real possibilities from illusions—no simple task.

If this first half of the exercise is successful, then it can be carried out into practice. With regard to events or situations that means that we try to make something good out of what may present itself as bad. Generally speaking, we learn from the given. This learning can be best stated by saying that one is to follow what is not good back to its deep roots in *oneself*. The question is, when did the given situation or story *begin*? The origin can be followed back astonishingly far. And then we look into the future. How can what has been cognized as positive be realized here? We must remember that this is an exercise, to be applied to specific events or situations; to investigate and transform our whole life in this way exceeds our powers generally since we are talking here of very deep cognitive experiences. Still, one single case, handled appropriately in the sense of this exercise, will have a formative effect on the whole direction of one's life.

Obviously this last exercise is very demanding. Above all, the judgment of negative or positive, which may be too easily made, presents a very serious problem: in the background there is always a more or less consciously developed worldview. And this may itself change with time. In the early stages, it is really a matter of bringing a certain degree of consistency into particular situations in life.

One's career is often a source of problems, even mental problems. Today, particularly among the young, it is rare to find people with explicit vocations, who feel gifted for one career alone. Naturally there are people who can only be pianists or doctors, but the great majority could be engineers, teachers, or bank employees, or for that matter sporting goods retailers, with equal facility. Our gifts are not so specific and the bent toward one course of life is not so pronounced as in former generations. For this reason, the choice of careers is harder and satisfaction in one's career is very rare. No longer do we love our work. Our interest therefore gets shifted over to financial or social success, and the discontent continues: career no longer fills up a life. Added to this, we now have more free time on our hands. But we seem to be able to do little with it, and so we schedule it very fully and it too passes in haste, giving us no rest.

If the choice of career is difficult because no one career stands out as preferable, or if one is already in a career that is not satisfying or not completely satisfying, and no other career is available that would suit better, then it is time to shift the emphasis in one's life and to seek satisfaction in another field. This is the reason why hobbies are so popular.

People who can find no fitting career are not less worthy people. They certainly have interests, but these are generally hidden. They themselves cannot formulate it, and it is not advertised anywhere. On the one hand, these people cannot discover what they seek; on the other hand, there is hardly anything there to discover in the wilderness of business other than mere busyness. Traditional rules and supports for life have begun to shift and sway, and this robs man of his certainty. If I have a burning uncertainty within me—*what is the meaning of it all?*—how can a career completely satisfy me? In former times, only certain "chosen" ones occupied themselves with such questions. Today, many more are chosen without knowing it. An evolution of consciousness has occurred, with positive and negative consequences. Many people are interested in this kind of question. Ideally, one could address such questions in a relevant manner during one's free time instead of practicing some other hobby. These questions are the other side of real self-knowledge and contribute to it. By examining one's own situation and that of mankind as a whole, one comes to self-experience: one knows oneself as the knower, and this removes all uncertainty. Then one's career, unsatisfying in itself, can be performed to the best of one's ability, without pursuing side goals such as self-confirmation. It is good to find satisfaction in one's work. But if this is not sought in the relevant professional activities—for the doctor, in healing; for the teacher, in teaching; for the cobbler, in making a good shoe—but rather in success, then the quality of the work will suffer. Success and quality of work do not always go hand in hand after all. For those people we have been describing, the time has come to concern themselves with general human questions: Who is man? What is fate? What is the evolution of the world? What is spirit? Or, what is language? One's career will not suffer from such pursuits—on the contrary.

To sum up: one should not undertake too many exercises at once—besides the general one, right speech, two others at most. Though one may have many failings and weaknesses, though one may recognize, or could recognize, many of those weaknesses described above in one's own case, still it is not the number of exercises that will make a difference, but the intensity and concentratedness with which those exercises are practiced. In principle we can be freed from all infirmities.

I and Thou

Today, man's past consciousness is egotistical consciousness. Through egotistical consciousness, man is condemned to *inner* loneliness, because being together, *with* others in a community, is only possible for beings who live predominantly in a present consciousness and form their social existence carefully according to the "laws" of such a consciousness. *Inner* loneliness means that we carry it with us wherever we go. It is no help to be with others, no help to be in the most intimate proximity with other people. The most intimate conversation between two people is still conducted as if they were speaking by telephone. It should not surprise us, then, that most people feel their loneliness and complain of it. Nor should it surprise us that they try to break through it by substitute methods.

At the same time, a tendency to flee from society, from other people, can be observed in those who suffer this sense of loneliness. It is a contradiction, but not difficult to understand. It comes from resignation: from the experience of seeing that togetherness will not succeed in any case, and the sense that it is therefore better to avoid even its external conditions.

By the light of the preceding thoughts we can recognize that man is a social being—much more so and in a different sense than animals—and he is social *through the word.* Words have meaning, even existence, only with regard to other I-beings, and presuppose such beings. When we speak, we speak as individuals, but language is the common possession of a people, and thinking, which stands behind language, is the common right of all mankind. Humans evoke this most general function individually: no one can speak or think "in common."

Today's societies, large or small, are rarely built in common essence, on the word, on thinking, which is a kind of higher word. Societies tend rather to be based on "needs," on the satisfaction of needs, and on egotism, and so their destruction is ordained at their very birth. Their rationales are common interests, business interests or opinions, membership in a family (less and less so), or attraction of the sexes. In each of these cases, the motive is egotistical. We want something. This brings partners together. But the egotistical law within them will separate them, in time, for the same reasons.

Even if a relationship—love, friendship, family—*originates* in unegotistical motives, it has to be consciously tended, these days, in order for it to remain intact and not die away. Tending involves a daily nourishment of the relationship through intuitively grasped possibilities, so that it does not become a habit, but is born anew every day. It is one of the qualities of words, and of human love as well, to have to die and rise again continually, if they are not to die out forever.

Because most of us are unaware of this, many relationships that begin will fall apart: marriages, love relationships, friendships, or work societies. External dangers, enemies, or difficulties can keep them alive for a time. But without creative activity, they fade sooner or later and finally pass away. This area of the developing consciousness demands individual activity, since institutional arrangements like church or state are now far from sufficient.

For man to be able to be together with *one* other person or with a group, individual as well as group egotism must grow silent, or at least be partially transformed. A group whose members bind together, forsaking individual egotism, yet shut themselves off from other people and groups, or even direct themselves *against* other people and groups, is doomed to extinction just as much as a group based on individual egotism. Egotism tends to divide itself up and to multiply. At first the group is inwardly peaceable, but then factions, parties, and subfactions arise, leading at last to the utter isolation of each member.

The exercise in positivity sets the standard here: to *know* what is worthy in the other person, and to know that *he* or *she* is this positive quality. Weaknesses and subconsciousness are there in every person, but they are not the human being. These are the very things he or she did not form and cannot control, even if the person more or less identifies with the goals of the subconscious. Analytic psychology shows man, above all, what he is *not,* what is not himself. Not that one should not reckon with another's failings—that would be illusion. But just as we do not address another person's cold or inflamed lung as if *that* were his or her personality, so we should not identify with a person those mental formations that are foreign, refractory, and inimical to the autonomous human being. Naturally, it is a difficult situation when people identify themselves with their illnesses and *explain* themselves *as* these illnesses. In such a case, we can touch the one-who-can-be-spoken-to only by indirect means.

We can ask how the subconscious acquires its power over men, over the human soul. By pursuing the question carefully, we discover "temptations," the desire to "do something good for oneself" in an egotistical sense, "pleasures" of various kinds. Some of these pleasures use the body, or its biological functions, as their instrument. The satisfaction of thirst becomes alcoholism, and the same mechanism works in smoking, which combines taste, smell, and breathing. And there are purely psychic pleasures, such as the satisfaction of vanity. The body has no mania for pleasure. These are all psychic "needs," and their satisfaction is more or less harmful to the living body. Psychic egotistical "joys" are often concealed by means of apparently quite unegotistical masks. For example, I can help someone materially, psychically, or even spiritually and yet experience a completely egotistical pleasure while doing so. It can lead to the point where it is more important that *I* be the one helping than that the person be helped. Naturally this calls into question the quality of the help. Satisfied vanity, ambition, or simple success are pleasures of a psychic kind that can be no less egotistical than bodily joys.

Joy, lovely spark of the gods,
Daughter from Elysium. . . .

Schiller was certainly not speaking here of the pleasures or joys characterized above. Behind them is always a desire, a feeling, that is bound up with a will impulse: something that may justifiably be called the *"outside* of the soul" (Rudolf Steiner). This has an effect on man because he cannot articulate himself within it, cannot identify with it inwardly, cannot experience it from within, as he can with a thought, which is all "inside" if it is in fact a thought for him, meaning that he understands it as far as possible. A thought cannot show me its outside, as can desires or feelings, which remain "outside" even if I dedicate myself wholly to their satisfaction and identify with them: I suffer them, I do not know how or why they have overcome me—*nescio*! Thought has no outside. It is *word*. Desires, pleasures, feelings of an egotistical sort, are *effects*.

This *nescio*, this unknowing, is nourished by the way in which we seek pleasures. "Satisfy your desires and be rid of them," could be better written as, "Satisfy your desires and watch them form again." Both bodily desires, which never help the body in any way, and psychic excitements, which have an effect on the life of our feelings and representations through mental pictures, tend to cause gaps in consciousness, and these in turn cause men to lose their overview of life, of the *whole* conduct of their life. These gaps grow larger with time, unless something is done to combat them and halt what causes them. In such cases, we speak of the descent of the person so afflicted. This can occur alongside an accompanying ascent in outer life.

The appropriate countermeasures cannot consist merely in asceticism, dehabituation, or renunciation of satisfactions. The energies that have bound themselves up in an antihuman formation such as craving, desire, or passion, have to be freed from these forms and led back to the *I*. Our whole therapeutic method is based on this principle. Those measures that lead to a dismantling of the excess of unhealthy pleasures can be grouped under the heading of pure perception. This is harder to realize than the preceding exercises. Therefore we can give only a sketch of it here and suggest the general direction to take. A more complex description will follow in the next chapter.

As epicureanism demonstrates, sensations and feelings of joy or well-being during eating bring no new knowledge to the eater, either of the food or of the processes involved in eating, whereas in, say, an art form we might expect such new knowledge to come about. These remain typically self-feeling sensations, even if the gourmet in question makes an art of being able to differentiate between tastes. We do not cognize the food being enjoyed, rather the taste organs are used to experience a psychically pleasurable feeling. We can therefore ask, what is harmful about all this, why should this be something bad? *Especially when, from another standpoint, it is so good?* We must examine the phenomenon of luxurious pleasures very objectively if we are to discover why many people today have the feeling (as did almost everyone a hundred years ago) that an extreme degree of such pleasures is harmful and something to be ashamed of.

We can observe several qualities characteristic of all pleasures. Such forms of delectation hold a person chained to one spot. There seems to be no path out of the dead end of alcoholism. The other characteristic is that such joys leave a person utterly passive; one allows the experience to flood through one. The model for this could be, say, ingesting chemicals that effect changes in the mental state without our being able to follow *how* they work, or to withstand their effects through conscious effort. And furthermore, the experiences of pleasure are unilaterally egotistical: one wants something for oneself.

If one were to locate these experiences within our inventory of the soul, they would have to be listed as *perceptions*. But they are quite different from ordinary perceptions, which are normally nearly free of feeling tone: what is meant here are not feelings accompanying perception as effects, but those that are experienced within perception itself. Artistic perceptions are different from normal perceptions. Almost entirely made up of feeling, they are still active, nonegotistical, and directed toward the thing experienced rather than toward the experiencer. Pleasures in the sense we have been using are perceptions that consist entirely of subconsciously caused feelings and emotions. Normally, man stands as an observer over against his perceptions: the experiencing essence, the *I*, hardly takes part in them at all. It is for this very reason that it can be the experiencing principle of perception. When indulging in pleasures, perceptions do not reach to the *I*; they remain trapped in the sensitive organism and tear the *I* along with them, so that we descend in these perceptions into a good-tasting trance. Pleasures are perceptions during which the *I* loses itself. And this brings to light another essential characteristic of these pleasures: a power, a force—here, perception—works on a lower plane than normal. Instead of reaching the *I*, as the perceiver, perception only reaches the person's sensitivity. And so it loses its word nature, which belongs to the *I*; it becomes *effect* instead of *word*. After having seen how normal feelings lure or force men into passivity, we should not be surprised to find a similar tendency in regard to especially strong thoughts of sensation.

Although the *I* falls into a kind of swoon during experiences of pleasure, addictions to luxurious sensation are to be found only in humans, not in animals. We leave aside domestic animals, whose forms of sensitivity have been disturbed by their proximity to man. For addiction, an *I* is necessary. Yet, in delectation, its effectiveness is switched off or weakened. Because the *I* is both necessary for this and at the same time repressed, we recognize it as an unhealthy function. It may sound comical today to call this a diseased state, because the disease has been accepted as the norm. But it is easy enough to recognize that these mental structures pull men toward animality, as if, through the abdication of the *I*'s proper functioning, a subconsciously formed mental beast were prolonging its life at the expense of the *I*'s energies. Certainly the origin, the why of addiction, has a subconscious source, and this applies to bodily pleasures as much as to mental ones.

At this point we should mention drug addiction, which has a special way of operating. The physical organism, as the bearer or mirror of consciousness, is worked on chemically and biologically. *How* this works remains unconscious; we may even be unaware that there is any effect at all. The pleasure is a psychic one, that is, consciousness undergoes a compelled alteration. The experiencer, powerless to withstand the effects, is then exposed to *psychic* experiences. These are mental or soul experiences; only a spirit can have spiritual experiences. But the spirit is incapacitated by the drug; its orderly connection with the physical bearer of consciousness is disturbed: it can no longer carry out its autonomous function, attention, the direction of attention.

The tendency for consciousness to sink to a lower level is widespread. We can even see this in the phenomenon of substitute literature such as detective novels or pornography. All these focus attention on content as opposed to method, on *how* we experience them. They are not there to communicate, but to have an effect: mental excitement, feelings of evil, horror, and mental pictures of activities ostensibly judged evil by the author and reader but which have an infectious effect because of the way they are formulated—an old trick, invented and much practiced by the Marquis de Sade.

When you can choose between Thomas Mann or Robert Musil or Huxley or Virginia Woolf or Proust, on the one hand, and a spy novel or television program on the other, which do you choose? Most people answer, "when I'm tired, a spy novel, a film." But there are many people now who are *always* this tired, or lazy, and make the easier choice: it requires much less activity, or none at all.

Every time the I-experience sinks beneath its appropriate level, every time the autonomous conscious man is relinquished, there comes a specially colored pleasurable feeling that is one of the characteristics of all egotistical pleasures. This quality is the reflection of another gesture: when one gives oneself up, in love, to another human being. For both gestures, the *I* is necessary. But in the one case it sinks down out of weakness; in the other case it gives itself up out of strength, and this makes it even stronger.

The other predominant trait of pleasures is the already mentioned self-feeling. This is a substitute for self-experience in the present. Self-feeling is based on a mentally overgrown sense of touch, which has a decisive, determining influence on modern man's whole life and view of the world: the real is whatever we can touch. This is a deep, tangible part of our mental outlook. Through the sense of touch, one experiences very little of the world—only one point, in fact, about which we know only that it lies outside the body or outside the organ of touch in question. Other senses, such as the sense of movement and equilibrium, are necessary in order to perceive shape, smoothness, or hardness. With an unmoving fingertip we cannot perceive either hardness, shape, roughness, or smoothness. But, at the same time, the sense of touch transmits a sensation to the part of the body that does the touching. This sensation is at least as intense as the feel of what has been touched, and is the bodily basis or sense side of egotistical self-feeling. The need to feel oneself mixes a kind of touch character into every sense activity: we "touch" a little when seeing, hearing, and so on.

In pleasure, the character of touch, of self-feeling, arises with increased intensity. Buddha mentioned the dangers of touch long ago in his discourses. This kind of touch is most pronounced in sexual conduct. And sexuality, in the widest sense, is the most endangered activity of modern man. Why this is so would lead us far from our topic; we content ourselves with the confirmation of a generally recognized fact. Because sexuality plays a central role in the life of the soul, justly or unjustly, we will now address it.

Although it is difficult for many people to realize, the driving force of what is sexual does not lie in sexuality itself, nor even in imagining a kind of enjoyment, but in the *search for a human being*. It is a search for another human who can relieve the seeker's loneliness, and drive away his feeling of aloneness or disconnectedness. This motivation can be discovered in even the most impersonal sexual act. In *this* respect, sexuality is a substitute activity and comes under the law of all substitutions: it is never quite satisfying. We make the discovery that even bodily proximity does not relieve loneliness. This disappointment can make us despise sex while still dependent on it, and turn us into people who renounce everything that set us on the search in the first place. It can cause us to look only for ephemeral satisfaction in the act itself. Imagination and mental pictures play a very important role in sexuality. The more this sphere removes itself from questions of reproduction, the generation of descendants, the biological function, the more the life of mental pictures will be involved, and the more it will be surrounded by a world of self-interest. This applies to every area of enjoyment and pleasure. A whole world comes into being from habits or social forms, and around it a suite of industrial products that serve these social forms. Our mental pictures are continually addressed and excited in this direction by advertisements, films, plays, literature, and pseudoliterature. If "normal" man has the sense that his willpower is controlled in other situations, then he will certainly make the discovery in this area. This experience contributes strongly to man's giving up his own humanity. Attempts to protect this area of life from the above mentioned dangers by means of consecration and sacraments (which at all times and in all cultures was undertaken by religion) have hardly any effect today.

In sexuality we have the most visible and pronounced form of a sphere of habits deriving motivation and driving force from the subconscious. Every justification attempting to explain this drive as biological is misleading. The source is not biological, but mental, as with all desires. The purely biological is as incapable of enjoyment as a plant; we use the biological as an instrument of our pleasure.

Now the time has come to say clearly that I am not an enemy of enjoyment, nor an ascetic, and I preach no asceticism. From the standpoint of the therapy of consciousness, nothing could be more mistaken than to simply renounce pleasures. It is rather a matter of developing more thorough perceptions, strange as this may sound; through these, we can experience a different kind of pleasure than through normal pleasures.

Pleasures are very incomplete perceptions, during which we experience ourselves or the pleasure in question. In normal, everyday perceptions, we notice hardly any feeling or will element in the perceived, although these are present, for example, in artistic experience. In pleasuring oneself, these elements sink down, becoming distorted into noncognizing functions. And so pleasures form a topic that we think about unwillingly, because that would mean drawing conclusions from our reflections. In his problem play *Man and Superman,* G. B. Shaw says something on this score. In a conversation between Don Juan and the Statue in Act III we read:

STATUE: But I am quite content . . . to know ,that I'm enjoying myself. I don't want to understand why. In fact, I'd rather not. My experience is that one's pleasures don't bear thinking about.

DON JUAN: That is why intellect is so unpopular. But to Life, the force behind the Man, intellect is a necessity, because without it he blunders into death.

Certainly man will blunder into death if he does not consider how he is endangered and the positive outcomes open to him —if he allows himself to be led through life only by his subconscious. And it is not difficult to realize that the sphere of pleasures determines a social behavior that makes it impossible for humans to live together. It is a behavior and an unconscious or half-conscious worldview grounded in pleasure, comfort, and egotism, which spreads egotism further both through the education of the young and through the whole way in which a life is lived. The exploitation of man and nature is bound up with this, and we do not mean economic exploitation alone. One can abuse one's spouse, a kind of exploitation free of any economical misconduct and yet still unworthy of a human being. Egotism cannot be transformed or set aside by means of resolutions, by will power, or through good intentions. Nothing remains for us but to tread the long, slow path that leads by means of an education of the perceptions to a more complete, and therefore joyous kind of perception; to a joy we normally substitute with "pleasures."

The Schooling of Perception

This schooling is appropriate for those who have largely resolved their psychological problems. It will harm no one to try the indicated exercises and experiments. But only someone who has few problems internally will achieve much on this path.

Language and speaking have become goal-oriented, utilitarian activities, although current research reveals that no known language was formed for such a purpose, especially not for the purpose of transmitting information. Languages contain the potential of being much more than linguists, poets, and writers have made them, a potential that was used during earlier evolutionary phases in the service of religious cults. And language originated in such cults.

Perception has had a similar development. Today's adults normally limit themselves to informational perception. This means that they perceive nothing more than what is possible and important for them. When surrounded by familiar things and phenomena, a minimum of sense activity suffices; I need barely glance at a house, a dog, a person, to know what I am dealing with. A very superficial glance is enough to identify what has been perceived.

If we compare this purely informational perception with a small child's, we see a vast difference in intensity. For a child, perception is an experience richly colored with feelings: the objects and phenomena of the perceptual world still contain feeling and will. Things "live" and "speak," are mysterious, friendly, or threatening. Child psychology and pedagogy are aware of the importance of perception. A dearth of perceptions prevents the child from growing spiritually or physically; perceptual richness lets the child bloom.

There are several reasons for the difference between children's and adults' perceptions. Above all, perceiving in a child is based far less on predetermined concepts, because these have yet to be formed. This is why the activity of the senses is more intense; everything has to be thoroughly looked at, touched, and listened to. Also, this intense sense activity is still intertwined with the world of feelings, and the feelings are still partly cognitive, that is, really *feeling*, feeling toward the outside, not self-feeling as in the adult. The wonder of discovery and the wonder of mental experience are still united. The capacity for devoted attention is much greater in children than in adults, and this is so to the extent that the child does not yet turn his attention egotistically toward himself. Psychic experience is multicolored and many-sided and can be characterized as joy, the joy of perceiving. This joy does not apply to the thing perceived but to perceiving itself. Or rather, perceiving is not yet as separated from its object as for the adult.

As is well known, children's perception, the perceptual world surrounding them, is close to, and has a deep influence on, their life processes. And this world is much more intensely experienced: food "speaks" to children—not only saying that it tastes "good" or "bad." Its qualities penetrate deeply into the sense processes, and not only through the senses directly involved (taste, smell, sight, etc.).

We can see right away that children's intensity of perception is replaced, in adults, by the sheer quantity of perceptions. These are a mere *substitute*: and quantity can never substitute for quality. Informational perception rules everyday life, bringing no joy. Adults take pleasure in the *perceived* (aside from questions of art) when "perceiving" for entertainment or to kill time, but there is no pleasure in the act of perceiving itself. Their lust for perceiving always remains trapped on the plane of information and in passive forms of entertainment. They want to be swamped with perceptions without changing the kind or the quality of the perceiving. And the attendant joys are quite different from those of children.

A justifiable question here is: where does the child's wealth of feelings and will elements disappear to? We can find these elements in the "pleasures," but in a much altered form: the feelings become extremely self-feeling, they no longer "say" much to us; that is, the enjoyer "hears" very little from the thing he enjoys. And so the whole symptomology of addiction to pleasures belongs with the problem of the feeling essence of man, or in egotism. Its gradual solution will be found in the education of perception. Such education would transform the ever passive "joys" (awaited from outside, external, and suffered passively by the subject) into an active joy that arises from within, similar to creative or artistic joy —a "lovely spark of god" indeed. Whoever has once experienced this knows that even the most intensive pleasure is only a pale reflection, like Esau's mess of pottage, for which we sell our greater joys too readily. To be sure, the path to these greater joys is a long one.

The schooling of perception begins with very simple, easy exercises that could be called trials or attempts. They allow us to gather experiences of perceiving.

1. One takes an object, either natural or man-made, and looks at it closely. Then one tries to make a mental picture of it with closed or averted eyes. One repeatedly compares

the actual contemplation of it with the mental picture.

Three fundamental discoveries can be made here. First we notice that we reproduce the object very incompletely in our mental picture of it. This is particularly noticeable when it is a natural object, such as a simple piece of flint. Its irregular shape, its veins, and its color will hardly reappear exactly in the mental image. A similar thing happens with the simplest man-made objects, while it is quite different with a ball of plastic, which has no structure. Therefore, it is best to take something that is not artificially made, such as wood, fabric, or metal.

The second observation is the abstract or *thoughtful* quality of our mental pictures. Not only are details left out: mental pictures do not orient themselves so much by what we have seen as by what we *know* about it. We generally picture a plate as round. Yet we see it round only when viewing it directly from above or below. We rarely see it as circular, and accordingly we do not *see* the pattern on the rim arranged circularly and symmetrically. The lighting is also rarely symmetrical, and so the *actually perceived colors are varied*, although we know they are really all the same.

The third experience is perhaps the most striking. With regard to the intensity of mental images, we are individually gifted to different degrees. The images will be more or less faint. In each case, there is something there in perceiving that is not present in even the most intense mental picturing.

Let us attempt to experience this element repeatedly and to describe it.

It is essential that these experiences be made for *oneself*. Reading this book is no substitute. We can experiment with the other senses as well as with sight in order then to compare perceiving with mental picturing. The individual differences in the capacity to form mental pictures for hearing, touching, smelling, tasting, and feeling warmth are very great. For hearing we can take tones (a gong or a musical note) and also speaking as our themes. To form a mental picture of a person's voice is already a complicated task, even when we recognize the voice with no difficulty.

These experiments show that each sense quality can be released from the object of perception and then taken up into a mental picture. What is missing in a mental picture as opposed to a perception is something different from a sense quality. For this element is always missing, independent of the intensity with which a sense quality is reproduced in a mental picture.

Whoever carries out these exercises will feel tempted to help along his mental picturing by taking notice, by intentionally "memorizing" while perceiving. One should resist the temptation and not try to notice anything. For such gestures of consciousness not only harm the spontaneity and fullness of perception—because we can only "notice" details —but also shift the emphasis unwittingly toward thoughts, which must be avoided. The point is not that one's mental picturing *succeed* or that it be more precise. It is not a question of a *result,* particularly not a rational one, but rather of exercising the spontaneous power of making mental pictures, because this increases the intensity of perceiving. Therefore: we perceive intensively and then try to picture mentally what has been perceived, without being concerned as to how far this is successful. We simply perceive and make mental pictures over and over, unconcerned about success. *Doing* it is important, not *succeeding*.

Despite their modest appearance, all these experiments have a beneficial effect, not only on sense perception, but on the whole inner life. And their relative unpretentiousness suits them for accustoming people to such exercises and to the joy of practicing. We must emphasize that every experiment is to be carried out soberly, objectively, while avoiding moods, emotions, and illusions.

Perception becomes richer, more intense, and closer to life the more colorfully we reproduce what we have perceived in our mental pictures. An exercise in concentration is also hidden within these experiments. The more these qualities can be lifted from the perceptual picture, and the less it remains abstract (because of conceptual activity), the more can be perceived. The two activities, perceiving and representing in mental pictures, strengthen one another. The difference between the two, understood as disparity, remains, although its quality changes. Reproduction in a mental picture is concerned only with *how,* with the intensity of the experiences of quality; never with *what* is experienced or with details. It is therefore best to concentrate on inexpressible traits, on irregular shape, subtle structure, and surface qualities of a stone or a leaf, for all of which there exist no words or set concepts.

2. The second kind of perception trial consists in noticing and experiencing subtle distinctions. For such experiments a cloudless or nearly cloudless sky is appropriate, in which utterly different blues can be seen in various directions, or the differentiated green of a meadow, the woods, or a mountainside. Using a similar method, we can take the colors of the sea, a river, or simply a tree that change with different times of the day. The same goes for sound qualities: the beat of ocean waters, the rustling of trees in different degrees of wind, or the noise of a brook or waterfall, can each be observed and reproduced in a mental picture.

During all these attempts it is advisable to insert little pauses. It is good to wait before the perception period with closed eyes, in order later to perceive newly, afresh, as if experiencing a thing for the first time.

3. The perception experiments have, until now, been given as applicable to individual senses. But in reality we never perceive through one sense alone but rather in such a way that one sense predominates and several others are also experienced. Beyond these, all other senses play a token role, as if homeopathically, in our perceiving. Yet, in reality, all the senses are always involved. This is most easily experienced in artistic perception. The more complete the perception, the more senses will be observably involved. The involvement of the accompanying senses differs fundamentally from that of the predominant senses.

Thus, the next step in the education of perceiving consists in the attempt to pay attention to senses other than the predominant ones. For instance, during perceptions of color, we can ask, how does it smell? How does it taste? Or, during preceptions of smell and taste: what color is it? Perception of form is naturally accompanied by the sense of one's own movement.* But we can also feel the sense of movement lightly touched on by perceptions of color, and by inner questioning we can raise it into consciousness: what kind of movement is kindled in me by this color?

The sense of balance takes part in almost all objects of perception, as does the sense of life. One can, for example, notice in experiences that combine form and color, how the life sense, the sense of balance, and the impulse toward movement are all touched. We look at willow and lime leaves, comparing them, and try to feel these senses accordingly.

An important condition for these exercises is that we do not fall into speculation or association: it is a question of our own experience, of *perceptions,* not of thoughts or half-thoughts *about* perceptions. These perceptions, at the start, are certainly very delicate, barely noticeable for most people. We should continue the exercises without forcing them, without *willing* them.

As an exercise related to the foregoing and perhaps easier for many people, we can notice the feelings of contraction or expansion experienced when directing the attention to nearby or distant objects. One will notice how looking into

* The spiritual science of Rudolf Steiner distinguishes twelve human senses (see Rudolf Steiner, *A Theory of the Senses, Themes from the Collected Works,* Vol. 3, selected and edited by Christian Lindberg, Stuttgart, 1980). These can be divided into three groups, the lower, middle, and higher senses. The lower senses are sense of touch, sense of life, sense of one's own movement, and sense of balance. The sense of warmth does not belong to the sense of touch: it represents rather a special *sensation of quality.* The life sense orients us as to the entire constitution of our bodily life, as we feel well or unwell. The sense of movement guides our movements. We do not need to look at it to know what form our hand or finger describes. Intended movements can be looked at only once they have been performed. Even biology is aware of a sense of balance and of the senses of warmth, smell, sight, taste, and hearing. It is part of spiritual science's teaching that man grasps vowel sounds or words through a sound sense and concepts or thoughts through a "sense of concept." It also teaches that the presence of a human *I* can be perceived by an I-sense or You-sense. Anything can be called a "sense" in this regard if man can gain knowledge through it without active reasoning.

the distance relates to breathing in and looking nearby relates to breathing out. We may guess that such breathing is normal and healthy in the life of perception.

Through these trials in perceiving, a new inner attitude toward ordinary perception can be achieved. This consists in the perceiver bringing nothing to the perception but his attention, awaiting everything from "outside." This applies particularly to all concepts. Still, this attitude is anything but passive: the "waiting attention"—that waits for nothing in particular—is the very height of activity. The attitude is similar to the correct one for listening to music. For that, too, we bring nothing to it, but allow the music to speak for itself.

With regard to music, this attitude is easier to attain because one is not tempted to meet it with concepts, words, and finished gestures of thought. But the state of mind striven for in these trials is only similar to the artistic state, not identical to it. The sought for attitude aims not at the *beautiful,* but at the *true.* It allows the perceptual world, particularly nature, at the beginning, to "speak" according to its "meaning," its "sense." For, in regard to natural phenomena, the linkage of perception with concept is only *nominalistic.* Really we do not know the meaning of a carnation or mayfly to the extent that we do of a spoon. The meaning of natural phenomena cannot be grasped with normal thinking. Even the sense qualities are conceptualizations of such a high order that they cannot be expressed through normal concepts and words. Therefore we cannot explain yellow or blue to some one blind from birth. We are similarly unable to express what a bird's cry or a lion's roar "means."

The attitude toward the perceptual world changes slowly, and it centers on the life of feelings. We have the sensation that the essence of the perceptual world is hidden behind a tapestry of habits, learned material, and conceptual reflexes. From time to time the tapestry pulls aside a bit, and the real essence of the world dawns on us emotionally. At such moments, the experimenter feels, at the sight of a natural vista, simply meaning, wisdom, harmony:

A flower's bell
sprouted early
up from the ground
in the sweet Spring;
a bee came by
and sipped on the sly:
these two must be meant
for one another.
GOETHE, Like and Like

The ancient Indians called such moments the sight of "suchness"—*Tathata*.

4. If the experimenter feels that a new kind of feeling is experienced during the exercise, that perception is accompanied by new, if subtle, feelings, then he can attempt (always and only as an exercise) to apply this method of perception to little innocent pleasures such as eating, drinking, smoking, and so on. Because man is much more wrapped up in pleasures than in other perceptions, this will be more difficult for him, and it is therefore advisable to experiment for a long time with only the lightest, most innocent forms of pleasure. The first experiences will show that pleasures take on new intensity through such attempts. The intensity is not of the same kind as earlier. One is to experience first this increase in intensity, and then to pay attention to its quality. The work on pleasures should always remain careful and playful, and be done a little at a time.

The intensity of sense perception grows stronger through a light, careful attentiveness. If we concentrate on the taste or smell components of perception during an experience of seeing, without speculating about it or trying to detect a taste by reasoning, then the taste or smell components grow stronger. These are present in any case, if unnoticed, and color our perception. The same procedure can be applied to perceptions of pleasure. Forming a mental picture of the experienced pleasure can also help to change its quality.

The alteration of our attitude toward the sphere of pleasures is of fundamental importance for the whole direction of our lives. Life is no longer oriented toward what is most agreeable and comfortable. Egotism, which directs our contemporary actions, feelings, wills, and often our thinking as well, can be overcome, and a new kind of joy becomes part of our experience. This transformation is anything but easy, comfortable, or pleasant. Yet it leads to greater joys. We can also call these the *pure* joys. And although this path is difficult, it must be taken or humanity will succumb to the consequences of a life guided by egotism.

5

THE PATH
OF KNOWLEDGE*

What Is a Path of Knowledge?

A path of knowledge is meant to lead toward more perfect knowledge or cognition. It requires a transformation of the *whole* being, however, because our cognitive abilities depend on our mental constitution, our mental health. Discussion of such a path is appropriate in a book about mental health, because the energies used for cognition flow into contemporary man of their own accord and he has to begin to use them or they will turn into hindrances to his life: *sub*conscious mental forms.

Cognition, however, has an as yet barely noticed significance for all of human life. In general, we proceed as if reality were finished, existing independently of cognition, as though it were a given that we know of *afterward*. We do not realize that we are always dealing with an *image* of reality arrived at through (indeed, made up of) unconscious cognition, and

* This chapter may be skipped over and read later on, should interest develop for such a path.

we subsequently face this image through a second, conscious cognitive act.

How far this second act can dissolve the world picture given by upbringing, at an unselfconscious age, will determine the reality in which a person lives. When we look at *our* reality, we have every reason to be dissatisfied with the cognitive method that gave rise to it.

People live in the same way that they cognize. Consciously or unconsciously, they always shape their world according to how they know it. Cognition creates reality in this way and, as far as it is creative cognition, it makes morality possible. Knowing, by itself, says nothing about what we should do. But it does determine the ways and means by which anything is to be achieved or avoided. Normally a moral act follows an act of cognition.

It is natural to ask the question: is everyone suited for such a path? Suitability can be determined by the following two questions:

1   Where do your thoughts come from? Do you form them yourself, or are they given to you?
2   Where do your perceptions come from? Do you form them yourself, or are they given to you?

Whatever the response—and precise answers are not easy to give—anyone is ripe for cognitive schooling if he or she can understand these questions. To do so, one must know what is meant by thoughts and perceptions and thus the consciousness-soul must be sufficiently built up to qualify one for such a path of knowledge. Unripeness is .evident when the answers to these questions betray misunderstanding of the questions themselves, in which case the criterion of the consciousness-soul, which should be able to observe the contents of consciousness, is lacking. The path of knowledge sketched out here concerns a further training of the consciousness-soul, which is already well developed in every normal person who has enjoyed a European or American upbringing. Naturally no one with a severe mental illness or prohibiting physical disease will undertake a path of knowl-edge.

With regard to age we can hardly suggest uniform criteria. There are old men of twenty; there are ninety year olds who are young. Much more important than age are the circum-stances of life. As a guideline we can say that only someone who stands in the midst of life, who has an outer existence, who supports himself physically, should seriously concern himself with cognitive schooling, and no one should take it up at all unless they are serious. The schooling of cognitive ability means an education of man's free soul energies and spiritual energies, which otherwise remain superconscious. It means an attempt to remove the obstacles to such a devel-opment. This schooling strengthens the autonomous essence of man, the creative, improvising, unfinished essence that is free of habits. We could also say that the training of con-sciousness strengthens the word essence of man in all its power, as opposed to his mechanical aspect with its finished forms. Man learns to live more and more according to his word. It is not a matter of cognitive abilities alone. These latter are simply a means for man's transformation into man —into man as he can really be.

The path has to begin with the education of thinking, since we do everything through thinking decisions. Even if we wanted to renounce thinking, that would be a goal, and it would require means that thinking itself grasped and decided on. We have seen how thinking normally serves nonthinking —the egotistical self. The first steps on a path of knowledge are attempts to free thinking from its subjection to our sub-conscious being.

When these first steps have been taken, one can then do further work on the areas of consciousness to which human-ity's evolution has led him: the limits of conscious experi-ence, the roots of thinking, perceiving, and making mental images. These roots lie *above,* as in an inverted plant.

Through these steps we must dissolve the remains of early, nonconscious education—all dogmas, prejudices, habits of thinking and of feeling—because these act as obstacles to the circulation, the free movement of the lifeblood of our consciousness. The above mentioned "dissolving" exercises serve this purpose. *The cultivation of a superconscious element, common to all men,* free of finished formations, cannot foster new habits without dissolving them and reforming them again continually.

The general attitude of mind necessary on the path of developing consciousness is difficult to attain, because it is so foreign to everyday life. It would be the ideal attitude for everyday life as well, but a different style rules there. This attitude is to be found today in artistic activity, and is as absolutely necessary for that as for a path of knowledge. To borrow the expression of Aldous Huxley, we could call it "active relaxation." It is the opposite of cramping, overexertion of the nerves, stress and so on. With cramped fingers or hands, playing music and painting are impossible. In musical instruction much work goes into loosening the hand so that it can transmit inspiration into artistic activity. Something similar can be attained in regard to gestures of consciousness. It is a problem of the will. That will by which *external* work is done is not suited to complete an exercise in consciousness. What we normally call spontaneity is the opposite of an act of will. The spontaneity sought in these exercises is not *given* to adults; they will it, but not with normal willing. In the East they might call it a nonwilling will. We can call it improvisational will. One does not know in advance *what* one will improvise, and yet it is not accidental, not directionless or meaningless. It is very close to play, and is a kind of play. In contrast to passivity, it is an *activity* that waits in readiness.

The way begins with *study*. This gives us practice in the observation of the phenomena of consciousness; we form reliable concepts of reality so that consciousness, the essence of man, and the world can be described and understood. We develop a kind of map showing us the way and orienting us with regard to the structure of man and the world.

Study is also necessary to avoid illusions or deceptions in our mental experience. On this path, much care must be taken against the dangers of illusion, and thinking must be wakeful, sober, and clear, that is, unclouded by anything that is *not* thinking.

It is hard to explain how to play the piano well, whereas we can say with great precision what a good performer must avoid. And it is even more difficult to describe exercises in consciousness, because everyone is his own individual piano, notes, and pianist at the same time. The only appropriate description would be one that dissolved after being heard and became translated into each person's own individual form. This means that the reader's intensive cooperation is being counted on here: a precise, sympathetic discrimination, necessary to understand these undoubtedly insufficient words.

Study

Proper study consists in reading—and understanding—works that treat appropriate themes in a manner suited to the consciousness of today: the consciousness-soul. For me this means, above all, Rudolf Steiner's works, especially his written works. Rudolf Steiner (1861-1925), founder of anthroposophy or of anthroposophical spiritual science, was a philosopher, but above all a spiritual researcher. His goal was to transform previously "occult," hidden areas of knowledge into a kind of higher science, and so to make them generally available to mankind, as far as that can be said of any science. In his works, he tried to represent the essential results of his research from two different angles.

His presentation is not simple, and his works are anything but easy to understand. This has the positive effect that readers have to become very active in order to read them at all. On the other hand, there may be no books as easily misunderstood as these, a characteristic they share with the gospels, which represent the essence of Christianity. Look at the variety of causes they have been said to justify!

The difficulties of communication in this case arise from the fact that it is not a matter of information being transmitted. There can be no information about the realms that lie behind the world of facts, behind the world of things and processes available to the senses, because these realms are the world through which facts, things, and sensibly perceptible processes *become,* the world of becoming. Information says: A is like B. In the world of the spirit there is no such thing as *is.* But there are also no fixed elements A and B existing prior to cognition in the spiritual world, and therefore no knowledge of such elements. All teaching based on the transmission of information and ignoring the origins of all information presupposes such fixed elements.

The spiritual world is in constant transformation, and, because it is the world of *cognizing* and not the common world of the cognized, it is also changed by every act of cognition. Cognizing, knowing, is a part of this world.

Our language is completely adapted to the transmission of information. It cannot be used directly in the description of the spiritual world. But it can be used to this end indirectly, in two different ways. On the one hand, it can be used to build up a world of symbols that *refer* to the spiritual world in question, just as written letters refer to their meanings. "Cow"—these three letters refer to a cow, without having the least similarity to a cow. But even a sketch of a cow is only a suggestive, transformed version of that which it "represents": small, two-dimensional, paper and ink, and so on. For an adequate understanding, these pictures must be "read," they must be understood "as if." Pictures do not offer immediate access to reality, but they can kindle soul spiritual experience of reality. Still, this is not an automatic process for the man of today. He is all too likely to use such images to construct a second world of representations for which he has neither the perceptions nor the corresponding concepts necessary for a normal mental picture.

The second method of description directs the reader's attention to processes of consciousness: more exactly, to the processes of cognition. Through attention, cognitive processes become stronger and the attention itself becomes heightened. The areas of the pre- or superconscious, normally hidden from everyday consciousness, become clearer, because the upper limit at which a process enters into consciousness has been raised. And so the practitioner of these exercises enters the world of cognition—the spiritual world. Experiences in cognition give him glimpses into the quality characteristic of the higher concepts. These are to be built up intuitively so that one may be able to understand, to "translate," the symbolic representations. This world of images, of symbols, stands in the same relation to the formation of normal concepts. (When someone's capacity for physical perception is limited, few concepts can be formed, or none at all.)

And so the two kinds of description complement one another. By studying descriptions of conscious processes that lead to inner attention, an *observational* power of thinking awakens, which first observes the phenomena of cognitive consciousness and then the hindrances, in consciousness, to cognition. In this activity, new corresponding concepts and ideas have to flash into awareness, just as with normal perceiving, otherwise no observation can take place. These new concepts, such as "living thinking," in contrast to the already thought, have an inner image-nature which has nothing to do with the image-nature of sense perceptions or their accompanying representations. The more this "observational ability" is allowed to be experiential (not logical) by means of concentration, the more pictorial these concepts will be, developed as they are in pure thinking. They do not correspond to objects, but to processes.

When, after this kind of exercise (because such reading *is* an exercise), the more imagistic portrayals are approached, the same thinking must be applied: a pure thinking, free from mental pictures, from perceptual elements, and of course also free from prejudices, memories, or habits. One tries, each time, to read the text as if it were for the first time. There must be no association. Through the previously acquired capacity for inner imagism, the images in these portrayals take their proper course: as symbolic tokens for inner experience, they call up the necessary corresponding concepts in the reader.

Study is an exercise and a training in pure thinking. It is called *pure* because it is free from elements of sense perception, from feelings in the usual sense, from prejudices and from associations. Today, man can use pure thinking in the areas of mathematics, logic, and geometry. Through study, he can learn to extend this capacity and apply it to the phenomena of consciousness. This means that pure thinking now includes itself in its ever more inward observation. This step, the inclusion of cognitive activity in reality, is the most important one to take in the formation of a new world picture.

It is therefore appropriate to begin one's study with a work written in terms of the processes of consciousness.* After a certain measure of progress in acquiring the capacity for inner observation, this can be accompanied by a work of the other, more pictorial kind: for instance, first *The Philosophy of Freedom* and then *Theosophy*. How one is to go about reading these texts can be suggested with an example in each case. To begin, we will consider a passage from the third chapter of *The Philosophy of Freedom*.

This is just the peculiar nature of thinking, that the thinker forgets his thinking while actually engaged in it. What occupies his attention is not his thinking, but the object of his thinking, which he is observing.

The first observation which we make about thinking is therefore this: that it is the unobserved element in our ordinary mental and spiritual life.

The reason why we do not observe the thinking that goes on in our ordinary life is none other than this, that it is due to our own activity. Whatever I do not myself

* Part of Rudolf Steiner's basic works are written in the language of the phenomena of consciousness: *The Theory of Knowledge Based on Goethe's World-Conception, Truth and Knowledge, The Philosophy of Freedom, Goethe's Conception of the World, Mysticism at the Dawn of the Modern Age, Christianity as Mystical Fact, Stages of Higher Knowledge, A Road to Self-Knowledge and the Threshold of the Spiritual World, The Case for Anthroposophy, Anthroposophical Leading Thoughts.* The more imagistic style of presentation includes: *Theosophy, Knowledge of the Higher Worlds and its Attainment, Occult Knowledge: an Outline, Cosmic Memory, The Spiritual Guidance of Man.* For a bibliography of Steiner's works in English, see *The Essential Steiner*, Robert A. McDermott, ed., Harper and Row, 1984.

produce, appears in my field of observation as an object; I find myself confronted by it as something that has come about independently of me. It comes to meet me. I must accept it as something that precedes my thinking process, as a premise. While I am reflecting upon the object, I am occupied with it, my attention is focussed upon it. To be thus occupied is precisely to *contemplate by thinking*. I attend, not to my activity, but to the object of this activity. In other words, while I am thinking I pay no heed to my thinking, which is of my own making, but only to the *object* of my thinking, which is not of my making.

I am, moreover, in the same position when I enter into the exceptional state and reflect on my own thinking. I can never observe my present thinking; I can only subsequently take my experiences of my thinking process as the object of fresh thinking. If I wanted to watch my present thinking, I should have to split myself into two persons, one to think and the other to observe this thinking. But this I cannot do. I can only accomplish it in two separate acts. The thinking to be observed is never that in which I am actually engaged, but another one. Whether, for this purpose, I make observations of my own former thinking, or follow the thinking process of another person, or finally, as in the example of the motions of the billiard balls, assume an imaginary thinking process, is immaterial.

There are two things which are incompatible with one another: productive activity and the simultaneous contemplation of it. This is recognized even in Genesis (I:31). Here God creates the world in the first six days, and only when it is there is any contemplation of it possible: "And God saw everything that he had made and, behold, it was very good." The same applies to our thinking. It must be there first, if we would observe it.

By carrying out the observations described in this text for oneself, we learn more than the text makes explicit. The "peculiar nature of thinking" seems to characterize other conscious activities as well: we forget our own seeing, tasting, and mental picturing when they are active. They are concerned with their objects and so are we. But—our first observation—they differ from thinking in that they cannot observe or perceive themselves. When we "observe" methods of perception and representation, we do so by means of thinking; when we reflect on them, that reflection is also accomplished through thinking. This uncovers a cluster of new experiences: we observe all the phenomena of consciousness through thinking. Thinking is what makes all pronouncements about these phenomena. And what is thinking itself—or rather, our past thought—observed with? With thinking. It thinks through what has been thought. These "afterthoughts" can be of two kinds: they can pertain to the content of what has been thought or to the deed that brought about that content. When we speak of the observation of thinking, we mean the second kind of these two kinds of observation. What can we observe in this sense?

If we look at the inner form of a course of thought, we see the traces of a meaningful, goal-conscious activity. This is all the more noticeable in a new, clever, or conceptually innovative thought. There is no sign of any "testing": it is as if someone knew exactly how to proceed, and as if the course of thought were guided, step by step. There was obviously no pattern, model, or norm to be followed. And even if there were, the authority that leads thinking would have had to know which pattern to choose. This thinking produces connections and relationships which were either not present earlier or hidden from view.

We can also observe that by "thinking" we understand a multiplicity of formally similar activities: simple repetition of a thought, combination, or bringing into a relationship several thoughts, and the creation of utterly new ideas. Finished thinking that has reached consciousness has a verbal form. And as soon as thinking is there in the words of a particular language, it is finished. If we observe the origins of this verbal form, we can see that it was not produced consciously. Not only were sentence structure and grammar *not considered,* but these are generally unknown, and no one ever speaks his mother tongue by means of grammatical knowledge. And generally one cannot say, even afterward, *how* a thought was formulated. Whatever directed thinking in its path is also active in the arrangement of words. Thinking becomes conscious in language, although language is formed as preconsciously or superconsciously as thought itself. On a higher plane, language must be aware of a prior authority—*before* the verbal form chosen in each case: should I say it in German or in English?

This consideration of thinking deviates from the "peculiar nature" of thinking as it appears "in normal mental life." Such "exceptional cases" are therefore possible. Small children cannot do this, however: only adults can look at their own past thinking—by means of new thinking. The center within that look cannot lie in the past itself or it would not be able to look at the past. It would not look at all, if it were past. The center capable of such looking lies outside of past thinking—in the present. But when thinking tries to grasp this present, it always comes too late; the present has just passed.

We feel our own thinking to be the conscious activity most proper to us: we are completely present behind our thinking. Our awareness must, and can, completely adapt itself to thinking. And yet we cannot say *how* we manage to think. "It has to be already there if we are to observe it." Thinking perceives itself, at least afterward; it always knows what it has thought. "To think," or to have thought, means "to perceive my past thoughts." The one who knows what he or she thought must have also been present in the *presentness* of thinking or he or she would have to think through a remembered thought again in order to know what it contained, and there would be no end to this rethinking. But for thinking to become conscious, that is, for us to perceive our thoughts, it has to be past, and formed in words. The how of thinking is just as unconscious as the how of speaking. Therefore, thinking and speaking have to already be there, in order to see from the outside how they came about. Their origin *in me* is and remains superconscious. This, their super-conscious phase, is their *presentness*.

These are *observations* that we can make, not logical conclusions. The less we have to do with the latter, the more a new pictoriality begins to grow in us, particularly during the contemplation of thought forms. It may be gray at first, or black and white, but soon something more like color will be noticed corresponding to different thought forms. Neither the forms nor the colors are memories of sense perceptions, yet we can hardly talk of them other than by means of expressions derived from sense qualities. We do not so much think as observe, behold, and see with a *perceptual thinking*. This is a new achievement on the part of the practitioner.

What we have described here is one of the countless ways in which the cited text can be interpreted. Clearly, a beginner will hardly be able to produce such results. The example is meant to show a possible direction for readers to take when they work with the text.

As an example of the pictorial descriptions of research results, we will use a brief text from *Theosophy*, from the chapter "Body, Soul, and Spirit."

Man, however, does not perceive the manifestations of the life-force through the ordinary senses. He sees the colors of the plants; he smells their perfume. The life-force, however, remains hidden from this form of observation. Even so, those with ordinary senses have just as little right to deny that there is a life-force as the man born blind has to deny that colors exist. Colors are there for the person born blind as soon as he has undergone an operation. In the same way, the various species of plants and animals created by the life-force—not merely the individual plants and animals—are present for man as objects of perception as soon as the necessary organ unfolds within him. An entirely new world opens out to him through the unfolding of this organ. He now perceives not merely the colors, the odors and other characteristics of living beings, but the life itself of these beings. In each plant and animal he perceives, besides the physical form, the life-fiilled spirit-form. In order to have a name for this spirit form, let it be called the *ether body* or *life body*.

It may strike the reader how much this text—as in fact the whole of *Theosophy*—is oriented toward perception. Analogies used to explain the life body are taken from the realm of sense perception. How can one perceive a life force? It is impossible to do so with normal senses. Instead, we perceive the effects of forces on perceivable things, even if it is a question of, say, electricity. Life force also expresses itself in perceivables: it builds the living form of the living creature out of mineral components. We can ask, is this the only revelation of these forces? The living form is not a *thing;* it cannot be perceived through normal sense or through physical apparatuses. The life form (called spirit form in the text) of a plant, for example, is the essence of the whole cycle of seed, sapling, growth, bud, bloom, fruit, and seed; but the idea of this spirit form also includes all possible variations of that kind of plant depending on the condition and preparation of the earth, the water supply, and so on. The idea is a process, and permits various possiblities in the world of appearances, which are limited only by the kind of plant in question: a buttercup stays a buttercup under any conditions. This spirit form is not visible to the eye or the camera, but it is a reality, indeed. a much stronger one than the visible plant, because the individual form changes and withers while the spiritual form includes both the changes that occur in the course of the year and the superindividual aspect of the plant. There are only kinds of plant; there is never such a thing as one unique exemplar.

If we direct our attention to the idea of an ever-changing lifeform of a plant, and recognize that this is a more powerful reality than the appearance of the plant itself, then we can see that this is a "form" in a quite different sense from the word's accustomed usage. It is called a form because of its particularity, which is the particularity of a *kind* of organism.

Whether a seed grows into a small, diseased plant or a healthy one, as determined by the environment, soil, weather, and so on, its *type,* its species, is not changed. Every gardener and farmer relies on this. The species is, for our normal thinking, an abstraction: the grouping of individuals that belong to this species (a formulation not without a certain humor). As we have seen, this species-determining spiritual form is actually a more powerful reality than the individual plants that grow and then wither away, while the species remains, showing itself in one individual plant after another.

The species or spiritual form is therefore an idea, but a living, life-giving idea. It is "fixed" to the extent that a plant species can be said to be fixed, containing a multiplicity of possible forms of appearance. This form is not a normal image, and therefore is not to be mentally represented after the pattern of our mental pictures of perceptions. Anyone who has worked through the text of *The Philosophy of Freedom* will sense the relationship between all this and the newly perceivable pictoriality described above. The new pictoriality that comes about through observation of thinking is suited to grasp the life body's spirit form.

Man can observe various species of plants in this way, that is, various spirit forms. And this suggests that he has, or can develop, the *ability* to "think" living ideas, to "perceive" the spiritual life-forms. This can only be the case if the essential energy of such life-forms is freely accessible to him. In principle, he can think anything, any idea, at will, while any given species has a specific idea. The formative energies that fashion a specific spirit form are present in man not only in his own particular etheric body, but in free, formless excess: this, among other things, makes him man. Living or present "thinking" is an activity in and with life energies. If such energies are bound to a form, we speak of an etheric body; if they are free, they can momentarily assume any form, during the act of knowing, at which time they may be called energies of cognition. In all cases (in contrast to physical energies), they tend to make forms.

It is clear that at first the images in the text were thought about through pure thinking, *without* mental images. A mental representation would obscure the path to the new pictoriality. The same can be said of other images, colors, tones, and so on. They do not refer to normal mental pictures and must be transformed, as in the example, and translated back into the experience they describe and out of which they arise. Special attention must be paid to *how* the descriptions are presented, because that, more than their content, expresses the essence of the experience.

As Rudolf Steiner often emphasized, the experiences he describes are not easy to reproduce, but their descriptions can be understood with a healthy, unprejudiced human understanding. Such statements will mislead readers of this book less than most, for we have seen how rare *healthy* understanding really is. Steiner was of the same opinion: "But this healthy human understanding has to be won through much effort, since it is not present today—it has to be earned by winning, through means made available in anthroposophy, that now absent connection with a spiritual world that was atavistically present in earlier times."* Anyone interested can find out for himself what high requirements Steiner referred to by the phrase, "healthy human understanding."**

Anyone who has lived, even slightly, with the essence of right speech will guard himself from speaking about his spiritual study without carefully considering that it is never concerned with *contents,* knowledge, and information.

All exercises and experiments described in Chapter 4 can and should be completed before beginning spiritual scientific study, especially the practice of right speech and the kind of exercise in concentration that secures the concentrated inner stillness necessary for the observation of thinking. These exercises can also be undertaken concurrently. Those exercises described in the next sections, however, should be practiced only after one has come far enough in one's study to be able to observe the phenomena of consciousness on one's own,

* R. Steiner, GA *176,* 26/6/1917. (Citations beginning *GA* refer to the German language editions of Steiner's works.)
** Compare G. Kühlewind, *Die Wahrheit Tun,* Stuttgart, 1982, for its chapter on spiritual scientific study.

and an image of the essence of human being and human consciousness has arisen.

The study never ends. In later phases of the schooling it becomes meditative reading and one takes ever new material for meditation from the spiritual researcher's reports. Steiner's own words show how he meant the study to proceed:

> Study is not ordinary learning: rather, one must realize that there is a kind of thinking possible for us that is still a fluid, real thinking—during which we exclude all the sense perceptions around us. . . . The human being must learn to forget and disregard everything that operates on the senses from the outside, yet without becoming an empty vessel. This is possible if one steeps oneself in a pure, sense-free thought content, such as what is contained in the spiritual researcher's reports, and then muses on what is developed there. In my writings I have followed this path; I wrote them so that one thought proceeds from another organically, as one part of a living being grows forth from another. . . . Whoever wants to rise higher must read the reports of spiritual science in this way. Whoever does not want to rise higher can read them like an ordinary book.*

This text can itself be taken as a theme of study.

Exercises of Concentration

CONCENTRATED THINKING

In Chapter 4 we already presented elementary exercises in concentration designed to strengthen the autonomy of the *I*. The awareness becomes concentrated, and this is the very measure of autonomy. When you *think* a simple man-made object, you make significant discoveries about thinking itself

---

* R. Steiner, GA 97, 22/2/1907.

and its hindrances—those factors that influence its flow, or distract or put it to a stop. The more concentratedly an object can be thought about, and the more unimportant and uninteresting it is, then the more awake thinking becomes. This wakefulness normally (in concentrated reading, in handicrafts, or in scientific and artistic work) applies to the object in question. When concentration is practiced as art for art's sake on an uninteresting object, then a heightened wakefulness extends from the object or theme to the activity, the thinking, the consciousness, *without* being distracted from the theme. This process brings with it the experience that the theme, for example, a spoon, is an "already thought." Whatever one thinks or mentally pictures about the object, all thought and representation, arises and has arisen through one's activity, whether it is a question of judgments, descriptive thoughts, or memory images of the object. One thinks about an already thought thought, a *thought:* the real spoon never enters consciousness.

With the illumination of this reality, one sees immediately that any man-made object has arisen from a thought or an idea; otherwise it could not be thought about. The idea is the functioning of the object, not merely the function of the particular one used as a theme of concentration, but of all such objects. All spoons realize the same principle and perform the same service. This idea is not a mental picture, because such a representation would always be of a *particular* spoon, whether fantasized or actually seen. And the idea is not a word, such as spoon, because anyone unfamiliar with the function spoon will not learn it from the word spoon. It was just this pictureless, wordless idea that the inventor of the spoon had. He could not, of course, remember a spoon and he had no word for it. We all took on this idea superconsciously as children, and for that reason we can recognize all spoons as spoons, regardless of size, material, color, or shape.

We can make this idea, the function of the object, into the theme of the concentration exercise. At the beginning it doesn't work at all, and we always imagine a particular functioning object (a spoon for ladling soup) or we try to come up with a thought-out formulation of the function. Neither of these is the idea. We can ease the transition to the idea by imagining a whole row of functioning objects (small, big, ladles, etc.) and then try to see the common element in them —the idea.

This requires pure thinking because the idea, the function, is not an image or a word; and words and pictures should therefore not be present in consciousness during the exercise, yet consciousness must remain awake, only without pictorial or already thought content. For normal consciousness this object of meditation is nothingness, yet it is possible to succeed and to think *that,* without it becoming a "something," a past thought. In fact, an idea or a function can only exist in current thinking, never as a past thought. Thinking, therefore, must never fall out of its process, as it normally does every instant, even during intensive thinking. That which is in consciousness can be an inner experience of light, or an experience of shadows in light, or a color, a smell, and so on. Generally this is preceded by the experience of finding that one becomes the object or the function oneself.

If the concentration exercise has reached this phase, that of idea concentration, as will develop organically from practice, the student is still concerned with an object. He or she wants to think the idea and wants the idea to appear, to arise, to flash forth. If this is successful, and he or she has learned to stay with it, so that it is not *only* a lightning flash, as it tends to be at the start, then the extension of wakefulness to the activity of consciousness will surpass in intensity all earlier experience. For in thinking the idea, activity and object are one: the idea does not exist outside of the activity that thinks it; there is no memory of it and it can never be thought out. We could also say that now we really know what spoon means. The self-perception of thinking has raised itself from past consciousness into presentness.

The idea, even of the simplest objects, is not a something but a happening, an *occurrence.* This happening we normally experience only in its results, for example, when an idea or an understanding flashes into us *through intuition.* We call this occurrence, as well as its result, intuition. In the exercise we try to stay, to dwell, in the occurrence of the intuition. The more successful we are here, the more strongly that new pictoriality we met in the case of spiritual scientific study begins to dawn.

This experience is pure thinking of a higher kind, a dwelling in live thinking, at the timeless birth of an idea. Because here the activity of the practitioner and the happening of the idea are the same reality, the light of consciousness embraces its own activity and therewith also the one who is active, the real *I*. *It is this I-experience that gives men sureness and security, which heals all mental problems,* because it is *experience.* Man needs no proofs, no confirmations or self-assertions of his existence. We can call this the fundamental experience of the spirit. In it, we experience how we can be conscious, think and know, without the words of any language.

In every kind of exercise, we achieve a first success with relative ease. The second success is generally much harder to reach. This is because, after the first time, the practitioner forms a memory, a mental picture of the experience, almost against his will, and he then awaits its recurrence. The second and third experiences will always be different from what preceded them.*

In the concentration exercise, the attention is directed to two phenomena unknown to everyday consciousness. The first is that we perceive, in the idea, a *happening*, a process. At first, this is like the process of lighting in an experience of inner light—at one stage deeper we call it understanding. With further practice we can recognize this light as *the* light in consciousness; whatever is clear, observable, even readable in consciousness consists of this light. The second phenomenon lies in a closer acquaintance with this light. It is not the physical, optical light which lights an object from the outside and yet has no form, no "word" itself. The light of con-

---

* On this topic see G. Kühlewind, *Stages of Consciousness*, Inner Traditions/Lindisfarne Press, 1984, especially the chapters on the "Fundamental Experience of the Spirit" and on "Concentration and Contemplation."

sciousness is word light; it speaks. The pictorial expression for this is that the idea is itself light; the light that illuminates it comes from within, for it is itself a light form and expresses itself through such light. It is a kind of speaking without words, that is, without the words of a word language. The happening, the lighting up, becomes *speaking* because of the light. This speaking strengthens the quality of inwardness in the conscious process. And this speaking is, at the same time, a comprehension, a hearing. Retrospectively we can say that it is also this way in everyday life: we hear, we see always and only what we do hear and see. There can be no question of a naive realism here. The things that seem to exist *before* our knowing them are results of a knowledge not yet conscious of itself, a process of knowing that we normally sleep through. We wake up normally only when the products of knowledge are already there. When man experiences the word nature of the perceptible world, the felt impress on the mind (whereby the world seems to be finished before it is known and to continue after it is known) itself undergoes a change.

Every act of concentration on an object throws light on the active consciousness. This light of consciousness or word light combines, in its unity, lighting-seeing, saying-hearing— object-subject: they become one in it. Experience gains inwardness and sensitivity through the word light, because attention gives new weight to the inner pole of the revelation-perception unity. We could say the word light lights within. The idea is in me; I am the idea. In this way, the practitioner comes to an experience of his *I*. By thinking-willing-perceiving the idea, his attention is lifted into the present, where a real experience of the *I* can take place.

Here we see the meaning of the attempts at perception described in Chapter 4 on therapeutics. While mentally picturing a perceived object, all sense qualities can be "lifted off." The reason for this lies in the idea of the word light: sense qualities are pieces of it. The object consists in this word light; the cognizing human mind clothes it in these pieces. Neither of the last two clauses is true by itself alone.

CONCENTRATED PERCEPTION

Concentration exercises for perception were described in Section 4.6. These can serve as the foundation of extended perceptual faculties by placing more emphasis on concentration. It is worthwhile, as a first step, to go through the whole palette of sense qualities—color, taste, smell, and sounds—taking each in turn as the theme of the exercise. Then compare the color of a flower or the green of a plant with man-made colors and also with mineral colors. Later, texture can be added for comparison: liquid, solid, and gaseous. Later still, the gaseous can be further dissolved into a kind of "warmth," during which no mental picture of the normal sensation of physical warmth should intrude on the exercise.

After the realm of sense qualities, one can turn to the observation of life: to observe the budding of flowers, leaves, saplings; blooming; fading; ripeness of fruits, and so on—all processes that have to do with the life phases of the plant. Common natural events can also be a part of this, for example, sunrise and sunset, or trees and water in the wind and in calm. In the next phase of the exercise sounds are compared: the sounds of lifeless nature compared with the sounds of animals. If possible, one should listen to animals that live in the wild.

After these preliminary exercises, one tries to *feel* the life of plants, their style and type. The same thing can be practiced with regard to animals, during which, when possible, we try to observe them in movement. In all these exercises one tries to pay attention to each of the different senses, as described in Section 4.6. For perception there is no stage that corresponds to "thinking" the idea in the thinking exercises. Because we do not know the ideas of natural things, or of unfamiliar man-made objects, these objects do not reveal their ideas to perception but only, if at all, to combinative thinking. Therefore in perception there is no middle step between concentration and meditation that would correspond to the concentration on an idea that follows concentration on objects in thinking.

In all exercises of perception, it is important to try to use thinking as little as possible. In these exercises, as well, concentration makes the consciousness more wakeful.

After exercises with types of plant life, the practitioner attempts to observe animal types. In this area, associations and preformed, even unconsciously active mental pictures act as impediments. All this must not go on during the course of the exercise. The most difficult are exercises with minerals; their conceptuality or idea is the highest of all the natural realms.

CONCENTRATED REPRESENTATION (MENTAL PICTURES)

As already stated, concentrated representation should be practiced on uninteresting, unexciting themes. Any of these will do. The exercise is being performed correctly if one can forget oneself as one practices, just as in concentrated thinking or perception. The everyday I is forgotten so that the true *I* can achieve self-experience. In this forgetting, the practitioner becomes one with the theme; he *becomes* it. This is hardest of all in the case of mental pictures, because it requires a double activity: a remembering of both picture and concept.

Representations, or mental pictures, also play a role when we think a man-made object. We can think descriptively about the object in thoughts, even thoughts formulated in words, or we can have mental pictures of and about the object. Both should be practiced; but to look at the object during the exercise would be wrong, because it is impossible to think and to see at the same moment.

If the exercises are done regularly, once or twice a day, the question soon arises as to whether and how often the theme should be changed. This question arises when the exercise has become boring, and a change of theme promises to relieve the boredom. But it will only help for a short time. Boredom appears because we are not thinking with sufficient concentration, or not *doing* anything at all. When we are really doing something, boredom cannot arise; concentrated activity allows it no place in consciousness, which is completely filled by the theme. The thought or observation, "I thought this same thing yesterday," is a frequent disturbance. When this thought appears, it means that the practitioner has made room for or allowed the possibility of this other thought alongside of the theme. Whether or not one thinks or pictures the same thing as in an earlier exercise has nothing to do with the intensity of the activity: in principle one must not give any room to considerations of whether the thoughts are the same or not. Thinking and representation should not be merely memory of what was done before, but current activity.

This point can suggest how far concentratedness is a moral question. Can a person surrender him or herself utterly to a theme, or are there ulterior motives, side thoughts? Concentratedness in this sense means improvisation at the same time, because in concentrated thinking it is impossible to work from memory or consult a notebook on what thoughts to think next. Thinking relies altogether on its present activity—it can only improvise. *Concentration therefore means improvisation.*

Concentration exercises in thinking, mental pictures, and perception should be practiced either concurrently or alternately, depending on the student's time and strength. But it is important to make all three activities conscious and to realize them consciously.

The time at which the exercises are practiced is significant. Special quiet times during the day should be used, if possible rhythmically, that is, always at the same time. At the start of each exercise it is appropriate to create a certain inner calm to allow a space for the exercise.

Meditation

Exercises in concentration are meant to intensify the conscious functions of thinking, perceiving, and mental picturing by directing the attention exclusively to the theme. Concentratedness changes the *translumination* of consciousness, and this in turn changes the theme: conscious activity and theme approach one another. The transformation of the theme is easiest to describe in terms of concentrated thinking: it extends beyond the individual man-made object and reaches the idea of that object.

This idea cannot be grasped with past consciousness; it belongs to an intuitive sphere. To concentrate on the idea itself is therefore an intentional intuition. To remain in the idea for any length of time is an unknown event in normal consciousness.

The deliberateness of an intuition regarding an object whose function is known finds support in our having "learned" the idea superconsciously in childhood, generally at the same time as language, which was also acquired superconsciously. All subsequent associated ideas take a similar route: the *original meaning* is never conscious, because it simply does not fit into normal consciousness. This is also the case with many nonobjective conceptualities, such as "beginning," "out," "hit," and so on. All these conceptualities are *used* by us without difficulty and without thinking about them; we say beginning in the most varied temporal, spatial, and abstract senses, because the primal idea, known to us superconsciously, makes this possible.

To express a spiritual relationship, language can only be used indirectly. When a truth related to the world of the spirit—to higher planes of cognition or to the corresponding realities in the world—is expressed in words, then our superconsciously acquired concepts and ideas can no longer help us to understand such a text. We understand a normal sentence by a superconscious movement of the understanding from word to word: the words must be neither forgotten nor remembered in the accustomed sense, otherwise no understanding comes about. We disregard the individual words, so as to understand the sentence between the words. Otherwise, hanging on to each word, we are like children at a certain stage when they can read the words fluently but cannot understand the sentence as a whole. This gesture of disregarding or looking away from the separate words should be extended to the sentence as a whole when reading a meditative sentence, because such sentences use words in an unusual way. Their meaning is determined by the meaning of the sentence. The meaning of such a sentence is like that of a word riddle, except that the solution of the riddle cannot be expressed in everyday speech. The method of understanding it is similar to the "dwelling" in an idea, except that we have never encountered *this* kind of idea before, not even superconsciously. The intuition here must be realized without any support whatsoever, and the idea is of higher quality than those with which we are familiar.

Such ideas can be found expressed either in texts (as sentences) or in pictures, figures: both stem from the spiritual experience of individuals. But all of nature also consists of "pictures," symbols, which express higher ideas. This is why we normally cannot understand the function or ideality of natural phenomena, but treat them nominalistically instead. We have names, but no ideas. Accordingly, natural phenomena can become themes of meditative perception. In what follows, we will consider meditation in thinking, in pictures or representations, and in perception.

THOUGHT MEDITATION

When concentrated thinking becomes sufficiently intense, we notice that words have become less important and that we actually use them less. Understanding is a continuum, and concentrated thinking approaches this continual understanding as it becomes denser and more concentrated. Language gives this continuum of understanding in a discontinuous form: words are a relative falling off from, or stagnation of, the stream of understanding. Therefore language, words, are particularly suited to the practice of "musing," an important stepping stone between concentrated thinking and meditation.

Musing in this sense is concentrated thinking that has gradually begun to renounce individual words. A relaxed but

175

very intense attentiveness pursues the theme. And the results of this attention must not be put into words. For example, one can take the word "out" and examine the whole extent of its use. Out means space, temporality, and also the extra-spatial and extratemporal. It has a twofold meaning as in "he went out of the house" and he went "out to the field": it can imply either out *toward* or out *from*. Think of "to give out," "outreach," "outlook," "live out a role," "out and out," "we're out of that," and "to set out." We find double or multiple meanings in many prepositions and other words. For the purpose of our musing, out becomes a movement, a "from inside to outside" gesture, and it is useful and easy enough to transform it into a *verb,* as when, somewhat coarsely, we use it as a command: "Out!" In musing, we try to "think" the ambiguity of the word *all at once,* in *one* gesture of consciousness, loosely, not associatively, so that the "how" of the thinking, its inner evidentness, makes itself felt in a higher form. Obviously, normal thinking cannot grasp a multiplicity of meanings, some of which are mutually antithetical; musing touches, at the very least, on a sphere of consciousness where ambiguity and antithesis become a single meaning. Despite all ambiguities, the meaning of, for example, out, is singular and specific: just as a type of plant is specific despite countless variations that seasons and planting conditions make possible. Musing is possible for nontechnical words. Words of relationship, such as "although," "or," "nevertheless," are particularly appropriate.

Musing concretizes a capacity that is developing today in all adults: the capacity to think without words. When thinking, which for the child forms a single unity with language, liberates itself from language, it allows for the possibility of translation, conscious lying, computers, and so on, and also for the growing accessibility of the capacity to meditate. Meditation on sentences, words, and texts can be characterized as wordless thinking.

Man always thinks wordlessly if he is really thinking, that is, thinking something new. First he has "something to say," and immediately afterward it comes out in words. That which is there *before* the words is closest to what we call functions, verbs, and especially *predicates*. In many languages, predicates need not be verbs. This observation can be the starting point for a technique of wordless thinking. An example will make this clear.

The suitable themes to start with are those that say something about consciousness or its relation to the world. For example: "Wisdom lives in the light"; "In thinking I feel myself at one with the world occurrence" (from Rudolf Steiner). "In the beginning was the word." "Man awakens in the word." It is important that the sentence, the theme, be comprehensible for normal consciousness, otherwise concentration has no point of departure for modern man. Words in an unknown language do not bring thinking into movement; the state of consciousness that emerges is not concentration but its opposite: dozing, associating, or daydreaming.

The sentences above are formally understandable for everyday consciousness; this consciousness could translate them, formally, into another language. Their meaning on the other hand is completely hidden; everyday consciousness cannot grasp it. Otherwise, the text would not be suited for meditation at all. Consciousness must elevate itself to that level. The words of a normal sentence force consciousness to understand the connection *between* the words, invisible as this is for the senses, by lifting itself up and touching the level of living thinking; in the same way, a meditative sentence forces consciousness to understand the whole sentence at one time. Understanding from word to word remains merely formal here, and the reader must make a single "word" out of the sentence, a word that naturally exists in no language. The words of the sentence only seem to be used in a normal sense. The transformation into a single word can be brought about more easily by going through certain intermediate stages. Let's take the sentence, "We always live in the light." To start with, the words of the sentence and the sentence itself can become a theme of musing. Very quickly, one sees that no single word in this sentence is comprehensible. What is meant by *we, live, in the light,* or *always?* We look for the primal meaning of the words, which means trying to think them as verbs. It becomes clear that the word *we* refers to I-beings who know of one another. *Live* cannot refer to biological life, because biological life is unconscious and not an experience in the usual sense. And the sentence would be meaningless if it were a question of biological life, because that life does not always go on in the light, least of all in the light of consciousness. The life of consciousness, which says *we* and *we live,* is also normally superconscious. If *we live* refers to the life of consciousness, it must be *realized;* it is not information. Meditative sentences are not informative: each one demands its own realization. The realization is the act of meditating itself, for which the sentence serves as theme.

We live is the conscious experience of the process of consciousness, and the process of consciousness is *we live.* Now *in the light* has already become light. We could also have begun with the word *light.* Then our musing would have said that even external light exists only for the light of consciousness, which is what is being referred to in the sentence. But this is a process, like all real understanding, in which consciousness revives, brightens, and becomes movement and life. And this process of the light is common to all men. The word *in* can also be mused over: to be in something, to be within, spatially, temporally, but also to be in the know superspatially, supertemporally. To live in the light means to become entirely light, in living consciousness; to always *become,* never to *be* statically. *Always* could be our starting point. To know about *always* always, without interruption, continually—that is living always in the light. All of this is musing. *Meditating* would be to realize the sentence itself, and that means to live it as an experience, to become the sentence itself. This makes the sentence into a single word—of a higher order, of course.

It is evident that, for musing, every word becomes transformed into a predicate, whereby we reach back to its primal meaning. This involves becoming conscious of that experience to which the word refers. *Word* means *becoming con-*

scious. House is not only a thing, a function, but also the becoming conscious of "that"—in quotation marks because afterward we have the experience that *it,* the meaning through and for our becoming conscious, "is" only through that becoming conscious, which is to say, it becomes. Anyone who does not "know" the function of a house, because it is not conscious for him or her, cannot *see* the house. He or she sees, at most, walls and windows, if conscious of these as concepts.

Obviously, a successful experience of *one* word in the sentence, followed back to its primal meaning experientially, tends to dissolve the other words of the sentence into the single word under consideration. *We*—experienced in the light of consciousness as a continuum—is already *always,* and *live* and *in* and *in the light.* It is the same with the word *always.* The other words seem superfluous. This is not so, however, because they determine the course of our musing. You can try as a test: "I always live in the light," beginning with *light* or *always.* You will see for yourself why it is *we* in the sentence used for meditation.

Neither musing over the words nor following the given example of musing with understanding is meditation, although it is often called meditation, not altogether unjustly, because it is certainly a preliminary meditation. Still, it is important to distinguish between the two. To meditate is to be able to *produce* the given sentence, that is, to really go through the experience which gave rise to the sentence in the first place: To make the sentence into a reality. Musing is only a means to that end. After musing over the words has brought a deeper understanding, one tries to meditate the sentence, that is, to "think" it without words. As stages on the way one can first condense the sentence into fewer words, and finally into just one word. Musing is very helpful here, and shows us that each word in the sentence could serve as this last word. At last we let go of the last word as well. Anyone who can think wordlessly, yet articulately, is meditating.

You may have noticed that the experience of individual

179

words resembles children's experience of their first words which comprise much more in the way of living meaning than is present for them later as adults. The general rule in meditation is to set aside all habits, meanings, memories, associations, and even associated moods. Concentratedness helps to assure that we are alone with the theme: this is why we must learn to concentrate as a precondition to meditation. Concentrated improvisation, as learned and used in concentration on ideas, survives now in wordless thinking.

What we have said should make it clear that to *represent* a meditative sentence, to put it in mental images, would be wholly inappropriate. It would be a gesture on the part of past consciousness, the very consciousness that meditation seeks to overcome, to silence, certainly not to promote. Even musing limits the activity of past consciousness to brief intervals.

Meditation is the experience of the theme. In the beginning it rarely works, not even after many attempts. No one should be frightened off by this. Even unsuccessful attempts are worthwhile stages if they are carefully reconstructed and thought over.

We can think of meditation as the search for a higher kind of content, a riddle whose solution does not lie on the plane of mirrored consciousness. Of course, even this search is not a gesture of normal consciousness. And the solution is not a flash of understanding after which we fall back into the "now I have it!"of past consciousness, but a realization or, more exactly, a realizing, a dwelling in the element from which we can normally only register flashes after they are over and done with. In meditation, it is as if a flash of insight *lingered*. For all this, the powers of attention, normally locked into feeling the body, must be freed and *controlled* by the I. Both goals are brought about by concentration exercises and by meditation itself; the liberation of these powers is also aided by a conscious dissolution of habits by means of the exercises described in Section 5.5.

The success of a meditation is an inner experience of understanding: it speaks for itself. Even the idea of a man-made object consists of nothing other than the willing human attention. In meditation, the idea is not given in advance, not even superconsciously: the content *becomes* real in the meditation and, because a *living* meaning lies behind the meditative sentence, the content of each meditation becomes "different" each time. The quotation marks indicate a continuum, internally structured, in which a word like different must be understood as inside the continuum.

Representation of the theme in a mental picture should also be avoided because it hinders the birth of the new kind of pictoriality as described in regard to one's study method in Section 5.2. Thinking a sentence without words, in a higher word-ness, is a structured activity, not abstract thinking. As in the simplest observation of thinking, when we see structure, forms, divisions, a previously unknown pictoriality, this appears in meditation as activity and process. For thinking the sentence we use not words, but this very activity.

A spiritual truth, that is, one referring to knowledge as well as to knowledge's spiritual object, can be expressed in the words of a language only with the greatest difficulty. The form changes according to the given language and so too does our musing upon it. For a less analytical language than English, "We always live in the light" must be constructed and handled differently in musing. The word *we* or *in* may not appear at all if they are understood by conjugation or declension, and of course the sequence of words may be different as well.

MEDITATION IN MENTAL PICTURES

A supersensible idea can be represented by pictures, figures, or even numbers more easily than by words. Supersensible truths are always ideas, albeit of a higher reality than those known to us, that is, known superconsciously. These images can be called symbolic pictures. Their meaning, as with meditative sentences, cannot be given dialectically. Nevertheless, they are words, they speak, and with such a multiplicity of meanings that for that reason alone the meaning could not be rendered in a dialectical text. And yet these symbols are very specific.

Such symbolic pictures do not reproduce a perception although they consist of perceptual elements. Examples would include the Orobouros (Greek: the snake biting its own tail); the Rosicrucian cross, a black cross with seven red roses ringed around the point of crossing; and symbols of the prophets in the old testament, or symbols in St. John's Apocalypse, such as the heavenly Jerusalem with its transparent cubical shape. Meditation consists in unriddling the symbol and taking its meaning within us.

For this, the image must first be pictured mentally—a fantasy image, because it cannot be *remembered* from our perceptual life. It is best not to encounter an external representation of the image, because we would then have to consciously dissolve our memory of this. Because the image is unreal and represents no sense reality, our realistic mental picturing is meaningful only because it ensures a preliminary concentration. When the image stands before our inner sight, then we can begin to observe it, to contemplate it, as long as we are not too concerned with the image visually. We can become inwardly still and allow the image to speak to us, just as with an image in the perceptual field. Generally, some preparatory train of thought is necessary in order to indicate in which direction to seek the symbol's meaning. Such a train of thought can be found, for instance, in Steiner's *Occult Science* in the chapter "Knowledge of Higher Worlds" in regard to the Rosicrucian cross. This train of thoughts corresponds to musing; if it were not given, we could produce it ourselves, with the same inner attitude as we described for musing over meditative sentences.

We can let the image of the Orobouros serve as an example. We imagine a snake, with a part of its tail in its mouth. As far as possible, the image should stand before the inner eye with the intensity of a perception. Once this has been achieved, we can ask, meaningfully: *where* is this image a reality? No snake does what the image shows it doing. If we allow the image to become an occurrence, a movement, then we can picture, for instance, that at first the snake merely follows its tail. If circumstances do not change, it will never reach its tail; the tail will always be a little ahead of it. For them to touch, the curve of the snake's body will have to change. Pursuit of the tail will not work by itself: if the head speeds up, the tail will fly from it all the quicker. If they do meet, then the picture can be considered differently. Beginning and end of a being or an occurrence touch one another; they bring one another forth. Does the mouth bring forth the tail and, bit by bit, the rest of the body, as if speaking it out? Then, finally, the head and mouth themselves come at the end. a contradiction, because they are the source of it all. If the tail and body are the beginning, if they bring forth the head, then the head can never catch up with the tail, which always precedes it. In either case, there must be a qualitative transformation between the tail and the head: the head can see and speak the tail, in which case there is such a distinction between them. Or does the body bring forth the head, which then eats it? Here too there is a similar distinction, but this one leads to self-destruction. If it is read abstractly, then it means: the caused brings forth the cause, or the caused suspends its cause, or caused and cause are one: on the level of the sense world, all this is a *circulus vitiosus* or a feat like the Baron Münchhausen's when he pulled himself up by his own pigtail. If we relate the image to consciousness, to our own lives, then the contradiction is transcended and also the necessity (not grounded in the image alone) of assuming a qualitative change. Consciousness brings something forth and "sees" it, and that which has been brought forth *is* consciousness. As we learned, it is no empty vessel. The image gives us self-consciousness as it realizes itself: at its start and then in its essence. We could translate the image, as it relates to consciousness, into a meditative sentence: "Intuition understands itself" or "Intuition is itself." But this relates only to consciousness. The image of this snake means infinitely more. Here too, musing is not meditation. In meditation the image or sentence *realizes* itself and becomes experience. And then we *experience* that its meaning extends far beyond what could be described by way of example.

The construction of this symbol, and concentrating on it, is a preparatory phase of meditation. The mental picture is not meditated, but its meaning *is:* the mental picture is only a cipher that points toward the essence. What this snake, the Orobouros, is, or the Rosicrucian cross, cannot be said in words. And it is not mentally picturable. The seeking and finding of the meaning is itself the meditation.

Meditation on mental pictures can be performed with geometric forms for themes, instead of symbols: for example, with a triangle (equilateral or isosceles), square, pentagon, and so on, or a five- or six-pointed star or a circle (all with or without midpoint). Without the appropriate indication to orient the practitioner toward that sphere of reality to which the figure is to be related, such meditations are too big for beginners, and we are beginners for a long time. That is, they are of such universal significance that the human being of today can hardly manage to live with them. Earlier, he met them within a spiritual tradition, a teaching, which helped him. This does not mean that he cannot work with these images, only that today some introduction is needed. He can try, initially, to meditate on the form of a circle, with and without center point, as it relates to the human soul. He muses over it: what is the periphery of the soul, what is its center? Which one determines the other? Can the periphery pull itself inward? Can the midpoint expand?

PERCEPTUAL MEDITATION

Meditation while perceiving is the most difficult of the three kinds of meditating, because nature forms a net of ideas whose filaments demand far higher levels of consciousness than are normally given to man, and because this net of ideas runs together into a single great idea, the "understanding" of which means the same as understanding the whole world and humanity in their mutual relationship: not a task to be quickly accomplished. This indicates the interwoven, meaningful structure of nature: finally, we only understand a detail within it if we understand the whole, since the function of the individual detail is determined by this whole.

This does not eliminate the possibility of perceptual meditation, though it does set a relatively modest goal to such meditations. The beings, phenomena, things, sense qualities, processes, and circumstances of nature can all serve as themes. Concentration of perception should lead to meditation, and the themes are to be arranged as in concentration. The first goal is for the theme to become an *occurrence*. Naturally, this does not mean a sense occurrence such as the movement of water in a wind: by occurring we understand a quality of cognition, as we already discussed in regard to the idea. If the theme of perceiving is a color, it becomes an occurrence when it begins "to color," that is, when its subsistence or existence resides in the lighting or giving itself or "the being seen," instead of its being the surface quality of a thing. The same cognitive phenomenon can also be described as the color's lifting or being lifted from the thing, as always occurs in mental picturing, but now takes place in perceiving. The moment a color lifts off or becomes an occurrence it acquires an inner structure, even when it is a completely even surface quality for ordinary sight. Painters do justice to this phenomenon by never putting even the smallest surface on a canvas without giving it structure (through brush techniques).

As a color can be lifted off, can become an occurrence, the same can be achieved for all things, even composite perceptual pictures. For example, with the image in Goethe's poem *Like and Like,* the flower's bell and tiny bee are already an occurrence at the physical level. The whole constellation here, the belonging, the Spring, blooming and buzzing, can be "lifted off," and only then is it the intended occurrence, the suchness, that expresses itself. The whole situation "lights up," in seeing of course, as it did for Goethe.

And it enlightens, too—a moment of sense-fulness. Once again, we are not dealing with the practical side: "How wise nature is; this way the blossom gets fertilized and the bee gets its honey at the same moment." Rather, it is a question of a meaningfulness that only shows up in the scene itself and expresses that there is a meaning behind the appearance.

What does the meditator do in order for the perceptual picture to become an occurrence? He makes the same attempt as with all meditative themes, by approaching them with the concentrated, questioning inner gesture: "What does it want to say to me?" The question is not merely formulated intellectually, which does no good, but is an inner attitude. It is just as important to bring a halt to every kind of clever reasoning, every combinatory movement. Only those who have learned to hold their thinking back from past thoughts are capable of bringing about this silence, that is, they who can *remain* in "fluid, true thinking"—in living thinking. In perception-meditation, we add perceiving to this state; it is as if one were seeing the image for the first time. In fact, one *is* seeing it for the first time. The practitioner "forgets" what the phenomenon is and what he knows of it: he simply sees or hears or smells or touches (but above all *sees* and *hears*).

When concentrated silent attention has been realized, other experiences also arise without conscious intention. The lifting off begins at the moment it becomes a "first time": similar to the way infants perceive. And so the perception *becomes:* the process, its theme and *I* become one, a single event. At the same time, or beforehand, an unaccustomed feeling can be noticed: perception feels itself, can be felt. It is a cognitive feeling, first only an intimation because the circumstances are not quite pure: *this* feeling at first feels itself as its own echo in the mirror of normal feeling, which later is still lightly excited at the same time. With further exercise normal feeling becomes altogether silent and now the exerciser feels his way into the perception, and the new feeling says more and more to us: it speaks ever more clearly within feeling. It is an artistic feeling: it says, not "pretty, unpretty," but "thus," as if the theme were beginning to express its *quality* in one vast concept.

This points up a further specific difficulty in meditation on perception. In other kinds of meditation the theme is given in limited, contoured form, as a sentence, symbol, or sign. In everyday perceiving we know where an object's limits are by means of the concept—this is the problem of perceiving on the part of machines. When we choose a piece of nature as the theme of meditation, we experience a similar difficulty to someone who has no corresponding concepts for perceiving: he or she cannot know where a meaningful thing begins and ends. In meditation, we must find that portion of the image, feeling our way toward it carefully, which has *meaning*, which can be lifted off, which can "speak" to us: the true theme, in fact. It is not a matter necessarily of a spatial limitation, nor must the limits remain constant: they can shift and thus the "meaning" may or may not change. We could say: if one "knows" what is to be perceived, one is already meditating. Naturally, this "what" does not mean anything graspable by the everyday senses. Again, the cognitive activity and its object are one: the activity creates it. A comparison can make this more clear. A student plays for his piano teacher. The teacher says, "Not that way: I'll show you," and plays the piece herself. If it is not a question of gross differences, the student may not hear what the teacher wanted to show him. It may be that he hears no difference between his own playing and his teacher's. He has to *hear it out* actively, that is, grasp the corresponding musical idea image: in this case, he must learn to hear.

The lifting, the allowing-it-to-become-a-happening, can be first practiced with sense qualities—colors, sounds. This would correspond to, for instance, meditating the word out, in the thought meditations. Then, step by step, we can take more composite themes: first red, then a red flower—a blossom at a time, then the whole plant, then perhaps its surroundings as well. In all these cases, even the simplest, we have to discover what the theme really is.

It is the same when we try to feel our way into a plant or animal species: these too are not given, neither as concept nor as perceptual object. "Finding" occurs by way of "seeking"—being open, being quiet, waiting—without knowing in advance what to look for, just as, in the meditation on thought and mental pictures, we looked for the solution of the riddle.

The pre-exercises for perceiving (Section 4.6), practiced with various musings, now bear fruit. And the more of our

187

senses that become conscious, or come near the borders of consciousness, in their otherwise unnoticed activity, the more the lifting and finding happens. This process could be called a "real abstraction" (Steiner), because the apparently abstract element—a species, for instance, or the high word essence of a color—is discovered within the phenomenon.

From the moment when the practitioner becomes identical with his perceiving, the occurrence grows more inward. In perceptual meditation this begins with a feeling, then an ideality prevails in veiled form. In thought meditation the reverse happens; in meditation on mental pictures it can go either way, depending on personality and on the individual theme. A feeling of the life of the idea announces itself. Normally man's sense of life informs him as to his bodily vitality, according to whether he feels well or unwell in his body. This sense impression becomes spiritualized and allows for a cloudy feeling of the theme, with which the person has now become identical. The *I* transfers itself from the body to the theme: attention switches its direction.

The occurrence, the lifted, found theme within the theme, becomes an inner one because the theme now plays the role formerly assigned to the body for attention and for the one who is attentive. At first the inner occurrence has a feeling character. If this feeling grows more intense and clear, then perception shifts from *seeing* to *hearing*. This applies even when the primary perception is hearing, in which case it now becomes an inner hearing. And so the idea begins to reveal itself. We could reproduce this experience as a thought meditation: "Seeing blue—hearing blue." In normal mental life this reality has its mirror image in the impossibility of any perception without some conceptuality. Even for sense qualities like color, concepts have to arise, in this case, out of perceiving itself. This arising has the faint quality of being heard.

Through concentratedness, perceiving becomes an occurrence made of sense content lifted from primary perception: an ideality in perceptual clothing. The practitioner becomes identical with the occurrence; the inner occurrence begins to sound, to speak: for the spiritual *I*. The "happening" becomes present and speaks in free sensitivity—for the *I*.

What is experienced through the *I* as an idea can best be compared to a style, a "how." But, in contrast to normal experience, the style, the how, is the primary and more powerful reality.

Every sustained meditation changes the practitioner's sense of reality. It becomes *experience,* not mere insight, that functions of knowledge are reality, and this experience transforms our feelings. Perceptual meditation is distinguished, from this standpoint, in that the practitioner sees the reality operating behind what is apparent to everyday consciousness. He experiences that the perceptual world *exists*—an experience otherwise unknown to human beings, since we only have immediate evidence of our own existence insofar as we identify with our own bodies. The rest of existence is normally experienced merely as a picture. In perceptual meditation, man experiences his identity with the perception, and there arises in him the evidence and quality of his being as he had not previously suspected—of a stronger and purer being than his own normally is.

It may have struck the reader that, in describing perceptual meditation, musing was not mentioned. What has been said about nature makes it comprehensible that musing over nature in the described manner is not possible: it presupposes special knowledge of the theme, particularly observations that relate to the theme comparatively and morphologically —as found, for example, in Goethe's *Metamorphosis of Plants.*

In the preceding pages, the first stage of meditating was described, as it can occur through thinking, mental pictures, and perceiving. The second stage, which was touched on particularly in the description of perceptual meditation, works with cognitive feeling, and the third with cognitive will. If the practitioner has progressed so far that these stages are relevant, he or she will certainly find appropriate indications for further development in the works of Rudolf Steiner or, preliminary to these, in my books.

Before moving to the second stage, the practitioner can already experience that he is beginning to read works reporting on spiritual experiences in a new way. He will come to know, in his own way, meditative reading, meditative listening, later even meditative speaking—the perfection of right speech.

He will also notice that many texts are only now accessible to him, for instance, the old and new testaments and particularly the writings of John the Evangelist. The first fourteen verses of his gospel, the prologue, is among the most eternally relevant and universal meditative texts, because it follows the development of man and the world, and their future perspective, in a powerful meditation. The prologue is a condensed statement on the essence of Christianity.

At the close of this section I offer a meditation, which could be called a meditation of temperament (*Gemüt*). It comes from Massimo Scaligero, a recently deceased Italian anthroposophist; and therefore it will be cited in its original language.

Conosci la pura gioia? Conoscerai il divino.
Do you know pure joy? Divinity will reveal itself to you.

But we could also meditate simply *pure joy.*

Dissolving the Habitual

Today we can hardly tell whether we have or have not understood something. The difficulty arises from habitual thinking, which is really no thinking at all, but only seems like thinking in a formal, superficial way. We receive new thoughts in the same manner. We can observe a certain modesty in the "understanding," coupled with an inclination to proceed effortlessly, when possible, along the easiest route. This attitude is utterly impractical and misleading, precisely in regard to spiritual scientific communications, as described in Section 5.2

(on Study). For this reason alone it would seem appropriate to carry out a fundamental revision of all the habits of consciousness that pervade our lives with a structural net.

We have seen, moreover, how the habitual human in us hinders concentratedness, hinders the improviser. For many people, concentration can only be achieved through exercises that serve to dissolve the habitual. By using the example of the most generic exercise, right speech, we showed that the exercises of dissolution can be deepened considerably, even infinitely. At the same time, we notice that habits give life a certain form, a structure, certain points of reference, and our renunciation runs the risk of causing an instability of the soul unless we take due care for the strengthening of the autonomous I-being at the same time. And so the revision of habits and the exercises in concentration must go hand in hand. The so-called dangers of a schooling of consciousness stem from imbalanced practice of these two types of exercise.

Our life is determined by how we cognize and by our activities, which are either required by life or correspond to our separate selves, our "instincts," our pleasure-oriented behavior. The revision in question concerns these life-determining activities, which can be laid hold of through a number of exercises. Some of these are given by tradition, and some are specially shaped for modern man. The individual forms, the arrangement of one's life—and it is always a question of the whole of one's life—are not of excessive importance because the work on *one* area, on *one* habit, always affects others as well, causing their dissolution.

Concentration and meditative exercises as generally valid exercises of cognition are the expression of a requirement for the age we live in: that man must form and further develop his own consciousness. The ideal is intuitive life in all areas. The intuitive, not the habitual, should shape and command those forms of which our life consists. Spiritual presence, instead of habits, should secure the stability of life. Spiritual presence means simultaneously intuitive *knowing* and intuitive *acting*.

For modern man, and especially for those who concern

themselves with spiritual scientific studies, *reading* plays a significant role in the spiritual life. This is new, as compared with earlier epochs. Therefore we begin the revision of habits with the exercise of *right reading*. Just as the correction of other activities in consciousness is briefly explained, we will also give some brief instruction as to reading.

RIGHT READING

We do not read in order to collect information, but rather to learn and practice *reading* in every sense. Read on any day only as much as you can work through, inwardly, in the time before the next reading. The slower you read, the greater will be the possibility that something happens to you during the reading, that something reveals itself. Learn to notice, while reading, what you do not understand: this is the gate through which you can go farther—a sacred gate. There are texts written by other than human hands.

This exercise principally concerns those readings undertaken as study. There are many distractions from right reading: reading out of curiosity, reading on a prescribed daily curriculum, reading for achievement, knowledge, and so on. One should guard against summing up intuitive or meditative texts, making extracts of them, or analyzing them. All this, as shown in Section 5.2, cannot go on without an essential distortion, without our missing the very essence of the communication. We undertake the reading as a conversation with the author, and so the "rules" of right speech apply here. One should never, even in other forms of reading, read more quickly than one would speak. It may be difficult with today's avalanche of technical literature, and *belles lettres* as well, but is is not important to read *everything,* which, in any case, is impossible.

When reading reports of spiritual research, there is a strong tendency to make a mental picture of what has been read. This is because one does not understand the text and seeks to use mental pictures as substitutes or supplements for the understanding. We have already discussed why this is a harmful inclination. When reading other kinds of literature, for example, novels, which present no difficulties to the understanding, mental pictures fall into the background: the tendency is to understand *only* the content, without putting what has been read into mental picutres. Mental pictures *should* be active here, but this is only possible when reading slowly.

Still slower reading is recommended for spiritual scientific writings. Naturally, we can only read slowly if we read deeply and completely. Such writings are especially many layered: they can be understood on various levels. It is like plowing: it can touch the top layer of soil alone or it can go very deep. If it goes deep, it is much harder work. And so the reading slows down, as if it were to think through all the author's thoughts that hover around what was written, and penetrate to the root of the thoughts meditatively. It is a question of concentration: the less concentratedly one reads, the faster it goes. A paragraph from Steiner's *The Threshold of the Spiritual World* can be read for hours, or repeatedly for days at a time. If you cannot read slowly and with sufficient concentration, it is advisable to copy such texts longhand. The emblem for our study could be Fra Angelico's painting of Saint Dominic: the saint is reading a book, but he is looking, not at the book in his hands, but just past it. He is musing over his own thoughts as kindled by what he has read.

It is not easy to find the specific books that are important for oneself. But those who struggle with inner labor can justifiably trust that they will find everything that would be helpful on the way: the books, the people, the career, and also the difficulties, the problems, the turns of fate—opportunities that are needed, even if they seem like unfavorable hindrances at first. This finding need not be considered as anything mystical, because the man who earnestly seeks or strives can count not only on his conscious abilities but also on his initially superconscious sensitivity, which, freed of obstacles by his first exercises, aids him in the search. The aspirant will read between the lines of life to find out what he needs by means of little signs that he would have missed if he were not on a path of study. We can also say that he is being led by a newly liberated, higher instinctuality.

The dissolution exercises can be divided into two groups. One group, with six exercises, was called a group of "supplementary exercises" by Steiner in his day (the main exercises were meditations). These exercises promote more general soul energies, which in turn make possible the more concrete soul processes, for example, the eight of the other group (traditionally called the Eightfold Path). The supplementary exercises can be compared with the current of breath and the other eight with the formation of vowel sounds: without breath we can form no vowels. Both groups complement one another harmoniously; they actually form the structure that replaces habits and makes possible man's stability (in life, in his soul) and spiritual presence.

The so-called supplementary exercises are as follows:

1 Controlled (concentrated) thinking
2 Will initiative
3 Equanimity
4 Positivity
5 Freedom from prejudice
6 Forgiving

The eight exercises aimed at more concrete activities originate with the Buddha, who also gave them their name. The Eightfold Path contains the following exercises:

1 Right mental pictures or right opinion
2 Right decision or right judgment
3 Right speech or the right word
4 Right action
5 The arrangement of life or right standpoint
6 Right effort
7 Right memory
8 Synopsis or right contemplation

The reader will notice that several of these exercises have already been treated in detail, for example, concentrated thinking and will initiative in Section 4.3, positivity in Section 4.4, and right speech in Section 4.2. The role of these exercises, especially concentrated thinking and right speech, has changed over the last eighty years. The general disease of consciousness, which has been described in detail, has lent them a new and special import. Still, all the exercises will now be briefly summarized (in meditatable form) and accompanied with a few observations. In part, Steiner's formulations will be used *(Knowledge of the Higher Worlds; Occult Science)*.

I   CONTROLLED THINKING

The practitioner should learn to pay attention to the course of his own thoughts, which should be inwardly controlled. One should avoid thoughts that hop all over like will-o'-the-wisps, that are linked accidentally and associatively instead of meaningfully and logically. The more each thought follows from the one before and the more all illogicality is avoided, then the more a cognitive sensitivity will grow. If we hear illogical thoughts, we strive to think them correctly. One should not lovelessly withdraw from illogical company in order to promote one's own development. And one should not feel the urge to immediately correct all illogicality in others. Rather, in inner stillness one should bring the inrushing thoughts into a logical, meaningful order and strive to maintain all one's own thinking in such order.

We see that the emphasis here (and it will be the same with the other already familiar exercises) is different from the thought concentration as previously described: but the descriptions have at base the same goal. The exercise in concentrated thinking helps us to achieve mastery over our thoughts. Concentrated in a brief time span, it can help us to this goal without our sacrificing spontaneity and fantasy from the life of consciousness. Every association to which we are tempted because of its accompanying pleasant sensations is a counterexercise: it strengthens the subconscious power in the soul. Nevertheless, outside of the period of exercise one should be cautious about interfering with the soul's spontaneity, even when associations arise. The more *spiritual* life takes place in a person, the less room and time and inclination there will be for association. Its place will be taken by intuitive, creative fantasy.

2 WILL INITIATIVE

Logical consistency in thinking should be supplemented by logically consistent actions. All instability in one's actions and all disharmony compromise the delicate sensibility formed by the exercises. Once one thing has been done, subsequent actions should be so ordered as to follow logically from the first. Those whose actions today contradict what they did yesterday bring into their lives as much illogicality, as much that goes against their word, as those who do not think logically.

We can learn to act in a logically consistent fashion through the exercise of the will—the superfluous activity (Section 4.3) that follows from nothing, only from the practitioner's original, unforced willing. Just as we must forgo associative thinking, we must forgo "associative" actions—those occasioned by nonconscious impulses. Again, nonconscious not to the content of the impulse, but to its origin. For the higher, intuitive spontaneity to be realized in one's actions, the life of the will must first be brought under the control of the autonomous I-being. Then, freed from the subconscious, intuitions from the superconscious can incarnate.

For example, we could carry out the will exercise in the following way. We decide on a very simple superfluous action to be carried out for a time, say, one to two weeks, at regular times if possible: for example, to undo and then rebutton a button. The performance of the exercise begins with our decidedly interrupting all other activity. We stand still and gather all our energies to pay exclusive attention to the movement we will make in the chosen action.

The moment of beginning should be isolated from everything else in our thought life and also from the everyday surroundings—so completely that it is as if we stepped with our entire beings into a vacuum. We experience the totality of our *willing* to make a beginning as it streams into our movements.

Touching the button, moving it, and everything further, should happen very slowly, so that the activity has to be flushed with willing at each moment. No detail of this should be imbued with the sleepy habit of movement, our automatic tendency, and no phase of the undertaking should be run through skillfully or sweepingly. The feeling should arise within us that the least detail of the action must *now*, at this moment, be performed for the first time. We enter into the "how" of this normally light, superficial action and attempt to master the refined touch of fingers and object, the movement of the arm, the extended time span of paying attention. The decision to do this act, flowing through the results of the will and the interwoven thinking that accompanies it, enters into the realm of accomplishment.

The moment of the action's ending should be grasped with a clear, concentrated attention. Later, perhaps, one can live through the beginning, the action, and the ending once again in thought, as if these three phases were *one* act, *one* impulse.

The first two supplementary exercises induce the practitioner to do something new, to carry out a new activity. The others consist more in inner behavior and in paying attention to inner behavior. While the first two limit themselves, as exercises, to a short time span, the others are more general requirements, which, however, may also be realized on definite, preplanned occasions. For instance, we undertake the preservation of our equanimity in an upcoming difficult conversation.

3   EQUANIMITY

The third exercise consists in the development of a certain stability in the face of the oscillations between pleasure and pain, joy and suffering. We should consciously replace the "heaven-high joyful, then deathly discouraged" (Goethe) with an even mood. No joy should carry us away, no pain should bow us to the ground, no experience drive us to excessive anger, no anticipation fill us with anxiety or fear, no situation make us lose composure, and so on. The feelings should be experienced: a happy event *should* make the soul rejoice; a sad one *should* give it pain. But the soul should manage to master the *expression* of these feelings. If this is attempted one soon finds that one becomes more receptive, not duller, to all joy and suffering.

The subject of this exercise was discussed in a somewhat different connection in Section 4.3. Its fruit is an inner calm that arises from time to time spontaneously. This is the foundation of the whole schooling. An inborn equanimity, or one developed in everyday life, cannot replace equanimity achieved by exercise. On the one hand, calmness in everyday life cannot guarantee balance on entering the more living planes of consciousness, or higher worlds. On the other hand, unconsciously developed calmness is almost always formed at the expense of the sensitivity necessary for cognition.

This exercise draws attention to storms of feelings that arise from unpleasant or pleasant experiences. A deep pain, for instance, pulls together into one knot the energies of the soul that would otherwise be active in experiencing one's surroundings, and puts the energies into its own service. The power that otherwise lives in noticing a near or distant environment loses its autonomy. One's attention to the pain is not directed by the will that normally lives in awareness; the awareness *is* an empty will. Awareness remains leaderless and powerless: this strengthens and exaggerates the feeling of pain, all the more so for the very sense of powerlessness. The soul can even lose its connection with the movement of the will that directs the attention: then nervous diseases appear. The powerlessness can also encroach on the sphere of the unconscious will that guides the spontaneous harmony of life processes: this causes diseases of the physical organism.

If some deep sorrow causes such a breakdown, then one should not simply suppress its outward signs. Concentrated attention should seek out the unmastered, powerless, immobilized feeling of pain that has drawn itself into an almost physically palpable point. The search proceeds by means of concentrating on the circumstances that caused the pain, by willfully thinking about them. And then the same will seeks out the feeling that was created. Usually we want to avoid the pain: in this exercise we do the opposite—we go after its essence. In a second phase of the exercise, directed toward the feeling rather than toward the circumstances, we can discover this feeling, now cut loose from its causes, and this means that the feeling has been surrounded with a cradle, a caressing hand: the attention, in which there will be no pain. The feeling, embedded in attention, loses its painful, knotted quality. It dissolves further and further and lives on in the soul as an unshakeable calm that embraces the entire human being.

An excessive feeling of joy can also affect the energies of the soul active in experiencing our environment—the will, the attention—and turn them into their opposite. The person feels as if he extended beyond his body, as if his limbs were merely following along. His words may also race ahead of his thoughts; he forgives everything; what normally causes a sensitive reaction now doesn't even touch him.

This overextension increases and exaggerates the joy caused by the pleasant circumstance. The joy comes from a release from previous sensitivity. This release is accomplished passively, and so is insufficient to make the joy into a lasting *experience*. The will for experience is absent here, and so the soul cannot elevate itself. The overextension is furthered by a hidden fear that the joy will disappear. For this feeling of an expanded existence is not a reality: at any moment some new event can make it collapse like a castle built on air.

A good mood can be a reality, and not an imbalance, if it has not developed through the disappearance of the will. If the mood has come about through imbalance, then the temperament can sink below its normal level and become depressive with the next unpleasant experience that comes along. Often no new experience is necessary: lack of power and lack of will make it sink back below the level of the more controlled feelings.

The less we consciously experience our feelings, the more they fall victim to catastrophes. An upheaval occurs as the forces of attention leap into a sphere where *experience* is impossible for man. No clear will informs this hidden intention. The overextension often happens through joy. It has even been generally thought that proper joy could only arise through falling into a kind of intoxication in which the soul's attentiveness is largely erased.

If the power of concentration can remain *within* the pleasant feeling, and not use this as a springboard for excess, so that this power can *live* in the feeling, then the joy loses its superficial character and becomes a peaceful inner experience. It can even help the experiencer to forgive and to deconstruct his oversensitivity and overvulnerability.

4   POSITIVITY

The cultivation of the power that lives in thinking, to which thinking owes its capacity for selfless application to circumstances, questions, and problems—this spiritual love—is called positivity. We can well understand this attitude of the soul from Goethe's version of a Persian legend about Jesus Christ. "The Lord walks with some companions past the dead decomposing body of a dog. While the others turn aside in disgust, he speaks with awe of the cadaver's beautiful teeth." This state of the soul is positivity. Ugliness, hatefulness, and error should not prevent us from seeking and noticing goodness, beauty, and truth wherever they may be. This implies neither uncriticality nor a closing of one's eyes to what is negative. The one who wonders at the beautiful teeth of the animal's corpse *also* sees the decomposition. But this does not prevent him from noticing what is beautiful. One is not to call bad good or make black into white, but evil should not prevent us from discovering what is good.

This soul stance will teach us to put ourselves in the place of unknown phenomena and beings lovingly and understandingly instead of judging them. And so we ask: how did it come to be this way, to act this way? From this attitude there arise true compassion and the effort to be of service when possible—as well as the power of judgment as to whether one can help, and how best to go about it.

Through this exercise, the sensitivity for what goes on around us opens and grows beyond the individual being's bounds. We notice much that formerly went by unnoticed. Positivity can be summed up as a means to transform the inattention present in every human. The environment becomes something that belongs to one's self. Concentration is a precondition for this exercise. Everything stormy, passionate, affect-ful, tends to destroy this new, outwardly directed sensitivity.

The exercise in positivity was described in introductory fashion in Section 4.4. The formulations given here serve for meditative contemplation.

5   FREEDOM FROM PREJUDICE

The improvising consciousness, in which the will to think ripens, must never lose its openness and receptivity for new experiences due to what it has already experienced in the past. What has never before been seen or heard should be met joyfully and never rejected. Everything, at all times, has something to say to us. Such an attitude does not mean that nothing is to be learned from the already known. Only, the already experienced should not restrict the new, and one should always keep open the possibility that new events may contradict old ones. And so the trust or faith awakens that the practitioner can master and understand any new event, at least to the necessary degree, and solve all problems. He does not cling to old opinions and experiences, but trusts his intuition and senses that he can change and correct his views and opinions. The trust in a new way of knowing changes into trust in a new way of acting. He can pursue his projects and his intentions with confidence. Failures and obstacles do not make him give up, but kindle new forces in him to conquer these obstacles.

The less man's past has rigidly molded his opinions, intentions, and habits, and the more his past experiences have given him *abilities,* then the more easily will he be able to absorb correctly what is new to him. Attentively avoiding prejudice, we see a sensitivity grow out of our accustomed life as if reaching toward new experiences.

The normal traffic of our consciousness with the world consists in feeling our own boundaries when a being, a thing, or an event comes against them. The movement of touching, feeling, curves back again in the direction of self-feeling, because the activity of consciousness can find no point of transition at the boundaries. We could say that it cannot neutralize the point of touch and free it from its self-feeling character. This feeling-one's-edges then increases and drowns out, in part or in whole, the encounter with the being or process before us.

The exercise is really a way of neutralizing and partially dissolving the boundaries of consciousness. At the moment of noticing, the moment of meeting, the moment when something happens, then generally some thought or feeling of oneself awakens, or there arises an interrelated chain of thoughts or judgments in regard to the matter at hand. The exercise of freeing oneself from prejudice precedes or loosens up the thoughts and judgments. It softens them, if they have already come about, and shatters any premature conclusion or hasty judgment. "This is how it is," we think, or, "Now it's like this." This step means that we actively *wait;* that we consciously empty the part of the soul where we are normally trapped by habits of thought and feeling. When this attitude succeeds, our feeling almost immediately begins to lose its hardness, smoothing down the edges that preserved the boundaries of consciousness. The point of contact with something new, an event, a being, or a thing, is neutralized. It loses the automatic character of a self-protective boundary that lets only information through, and the contact becomes

primarily an experience of style. Meeting something new—
and *everything* becomes new—no longer takes place in one
point, but in a line, a plane, a whole space, that embraces the
experiencer, the experience, the event, the thing, or the being
in a single unity without bounds.

6 FORGIVING

If we regularly alternate the five exercises described above,
an equilibrium develops within the soul. Dissatisfaction with
either the appearance or the essence of the world disappears.
Gradually, a *forgiving* mood awakens that is the opposite of
indifference. It makes it possible to work for the progress of
the world and improve it practically. There opens within us
a calm comprehension of things that had been closed off
from the soul. At the same time, patience and tolerance
awaken in regard to people, other creatures, and events. The
practitioner is to avoid everything *superfluous*, all self-com-
placency, and all criticism of imperfection or evil, trying instead to understand these things. He does not withdraw his
understanding participation, but tries to put himself in the
other person's place and find out how to help him.

Regular practice of the sixth exercise puts the soul in touch
with an energy that can be, for example, "directed" toward
the attention. This helps develop the soul's independence
from psychic reactivity.

This reactivity is not an element of presentness; it is rather
a compensatory movement to the rapid evanescense, the
past-oriented character of events and thoughts: a counterac-
tion. The self-strengthening will mentioned in the fifth exercise *is* present: a will of the human presence.

This means that one's sensitivity becomes a sense organ for
touching the world. The appearance of a force we ourselves
can direct tends to establish the connection with everything
the soul, in its egotistical sensitivity, has turned away from,
brushed aside, and not been able to absorb.

In the sixth exercise, the human being tries to activate his
consciousness according to the nature of a directable force.

Thinking will be prepared to detach itself from apparently concrete information, to further differentiate itself, and to let itself be formed along the lines of previously unguessed-at relationships as these latter may require. It will continually be ready to come loose and then go on weaving itself further. Nothing is lost to it; this thinking finds everything to be of worth; nothing is underestimated, nothing rejected. The life of feeling changes accordingly: to the extent that it becomes independent of psychic reactivity, it builds up a new system of sense organs through whose sensitivity the soul is woven together even with its previously alienated environment.

The soul willingly throws off its thousand-year-old habits of feeling: vanity, jealousy, vengefulness, and so on. Unceasing labor gives birth to the true human smile as the first stage of wisdom. The soul sees the world in new colors. It willingly takes part in the taking place of things, events, facts; and the fruits of this activity beam their ripe redness far and wide.

The forces of the soul and the types of soul constitution developed in the six supplementary exercises are like the warp of a weaving. The woof corresponds to the activities of the soul on the Eightfold Path. These exercises were formulated for modern man by Rudolf Steiner.* They seem to suggest behaviors that are actually obvious to any cultured person. But their strict realization will hardly be possible—today less than ever—without specific exercises. The following descriptions, which follow R. Steiner's formulation, are to be considered sketches: filling them out for oneself is the first step in the exercise.

I   RIGHT MENTAL PICTURES OR RIGHT OPINION

The first exercise consists in directing our care and attention to our mental pictures, or representations, and to how these are formed. Normally a person allows all this to be governed purely by chance. He hears and sees this or that, and a cor-

* Compare G. Kühlewind, *Die Diener des Logos* (Appendix), Stuttgart, 1981.

responding mental picture forms within him. In this way his cognizing can never evolve. He must educate himself in this regard. He must learn to pay attention to his mental pictures, seeing in them a report about the outer world. And he must not rest content with mental pictures devoid of this significance. He should develop his whole conceptual world in such a way that it becomes a faithful mirror of the external world, and, accordingly, strive to eliminate all incorrect mental pictures from the soul. He should make an effort to distinguish gradually between the essential and the inessential, between the ephemeral and the eternal, between truth and mere opinion in his thought life. He is to try to remain inwardly silent when listening to others speak, and to renounce both all concurrence and all negative criticism, even in terms of thinking and feeling.

Human beings are not accustomed to examining the correctness of their mental pictures, even though these often arise prematurely, under the influence of sympathy and antipathy. Concentration in thinking teaches us the possibility of forming mental pictures by will alone. When forming a mental picture as a result of some impression, we should exclude nonconscious, spontaneous formations just as during the concentration exercise. When I do reach the right mental picture of a thing it results in a certain feeling: that I am becoming identical with the truth relating to this matter, identical with its discovery, with its being. A falsely formed mental picture gives rise to a lasting, unpleasant, energy-wasting tension, as long as the fact in question is not *utterly* locked up in the false image. And then a suite of further false mental pictures builds onward from the first.

The requirement to distinguish the eternal from the ephemeral, and truth from subjective opinion, seems at first to be a very lofty commandment. But the soul's deep movement toward life tends toward these distinctions, because to find them is its proper physic and balm.

The *formation* of an opinion or mental picture should not be accompanied by feelings. Mental pictures formed independently of spontaneous feelings can then kindle the right, appropriate feelings, which are in harmony and identity with the truth. Actually, only truth should awaken feelings: *harmony between one's feelings and the truth leads to the healing of all the disease and suffering that plague and burden mankind.*

2   RIGHT DECISION OR RIGHT JUDGMENT

The second soul process to be worked on is the way in which we make decisions. Even decisions to do something unimportant should be well considered. All thoughtless, senseless activity should be avoided; one acts only on well-balanced grounds and omits actions prompted by unimportant motives. If convinced of the correctness of a decision, one should hold to it with inner steadfastness. This is the so-called right judgment, which cannot depend on sympathy or antipathy.

People often act without having made a conscious decision to do so, and they often act *against* their decisions. To notice this, to pay attention to it, is the first step in this exercise, through which we learn to act by conscious decision. This has its source in judgment, in judging circumstances. The capacity for judgment that we practice can be intuitive—a spiritual presence—and the more the practitioner behaves strictly in line with his decisions, the more certainty will operate in his capacity for judgment. Acting against one's decisions, against one's own judgment, compromises this ability —particularly if it goes unnoticed or if the judgment, the decision, is subsequently changed to justify one's actions.

Nevertheless, it would not be appropriate to banish all playfulness from life. But a person should know: "Now I am playing." If one acts against one's own insight, then the sources of the driving impulse should be pursued, examined, and not extenuated. One should neither dwell in illusions as to the subconscious impulses, nor justify them in one's thoughts. If they are obeyed, then this should at least go on consciously, which is not a comfortable state.

Out of the battle between our judgment and other impulses, a love for the power of judgment can arise that no one would want to do without once he has experienced it.

Allowing the capacity for judgment to function gives birth to this love, which in turn heightens the capacity. This capacity then turns more and more into spiritual presence, into the bright liveliness of the power of judgment—to which the love applies, and with which it is man's innermost desire to work in unison.

3 RIGHT SPEECH OR THE RIGHT WORD

The third process is speech. *One is to speak only if one truly has something to say.* In this sense, all talking just for the sake of talking, for example, to pass the time, is harmful because it distracts the practitioner from his path. The normal manner of conversation, in which everything gets talked about in a colorful confusion, should be avoided, but one should not exclude oneself from contact with one's fellows. Speaking should gradually develop its proper significance during just such contact. One speaks to and answers anyone, but always thoughtfully and with proper consideration. Instead of speaking to no purpose, one is willing to remain silent. One attempts to use neither too many nor too few words. The speech of others should be listened to calmly, and then worked with.

Much was discussed as to right speech in Section 4.2. If the exercise is deepened in a meditative direction, then we experience that this exercise really contains all the others: concentration, positivity, right representation, decision, standpoint, memory, and so on. It leads to consciousness of language as a phenomenon; one follows the individual words back to their source, to their original meaning, and attempts to find the *right words* for natural phenomena normally named only from the outside: their meaning, their function in the world.

The path leads on from this exercise to a new formation of society: through cultivation of the wordless word, which weaves through meditation and which, in its presentness, is the first new spiritual zone common to all.*

* Compare G. Kühlewind, *Die Diener des Logos*, Chapters X, XI, XII, Stuttgart, 1981.

4 RIGHT ACTION

The fourth exercise concerns the regulation of external actions. These should not be disruptive to our fellow man. What we do should blend in harmoniously with our environment, our life situation, and so on. If we are induced to act by some outside agent, we should take care as to how we can best complete the task at hand. If we act from our own impulse, then we weigh exactly the effects of our actions, even from the point of view of mankind as a whole.

A human being's external deeds are the consequence of his words. They are wordlike, to the extent that they are *human* deeds. This is why they are of interest to humanity, generally even when this seems impossible. Because deeds are words, are utterance, they should be treated as right speech, emerging from a clarity of intention and completed through a clear deliberation on how to behave. In the ideal case, deeds, like right words, unite heaven and earth.

To act, and to speak autonomous words: it is for this that man was given the earth and his earthly life. Elsewhere he would be incapable of it. And so earthly activity can give rise to pure joy.

When moved to act by another person or by external circumstances, we should consider the deed long enough so that from our musing an initiative of our own is born. Clarity of intention should weave through and illumine the entire action; in this way, it can transmit and represent the word nature of the world, both to the actor and to others.

5 ARRANGEMENT OF LIFE OR RIGHT STANDPOINT

The fifth aspect is the arrangement of the entire life. We try to live according to nature and according to the spirit, and not to let ourselves be determined by our compulsions or superficialities. We avoid everything that brings haste and unrest into our lives. Nothing should rush us, but we should not be sluggish either. The human being is to regard life as a means and opportunity for work, for further evolution, and to act accordingly. He arranges the care of his health and habits so that they result in a harmonious life.

A basic spiritual law stands at the background of the exercise: "I-beings can only exist if they continually evolve further, climbing higher on the ladder of creation." They have no permanent, static existence like creatures in nature or man-made objects. If an I-being does not develop upward, in the direction of the (initially superconscious) sources of consciousness, then it sickens, sinks, and decays. One's further development therefore has a goal that contradicts egotism: it leads to the birth of the *true I*.

This point of view should pervade the whole arrangement of one's life, and life should have such a consciously formed arrangement, because only the rarest of humans will live spontaneously from the standpoint of their own further development. Life is far more likely to degenerate into laziness, complacency, and egotistical pleasure seeking.

6   RIGHT EFFORT

The sixth aspect is the direction of human effort. One examines his abilities, his knowledge, and lives accordingly. One takes care to do nothing beyond one's powers, but also to omit nothing that lies within one's capacity to achieve. One looks beyond the everyday, the momentary, and sets oneself goals and ideals that are beneficial to the health and further evolution of mankind. This can be summed up as letting all the previous exercises become habitual.

This exercise summons us to a further step within the arrangement of life. That exercise drew one's gaze toward the general forming of the life, while this concerns the more concrete direction of one's efforts according to one's phase of development.

7   RIGHT MEMORY

The seventh aspect of the life of the soul is for the person to make an effort to learn as much as possible from life. Everything can be the occasion for conscious experiences that are helpful to us in further forming our lives. One should picture to oneself exactly how one has neglected something, and how it should have been done. One should observe the actions of others with the same intention, but not with a loveless criticality. A great deal can be learned from each human being, and particularly from children, if one pays attention. This exercise is also called *right remembrance;* we remember what we have learned and the experiences we have undergone.

8   SYNOPSIS OR RIGHT CONTEMPLATION

Finally, the eighth exercise is this: to look within from time to time and test how far we have succeeded in following our own life principles—what is to be changed in this respect and how the change can be achieved. From the field of many failures and weaknesses, we designate one as the next to be conquered. Special attention should be turned toward inner responsibility, toward one's honesty to oneself. One considers how one's own life stands in regard to the totality of human goals. This exercise has also been called *right contemplation.*

Contemplation directs the inner gaze toward the struggle that goes on continually in every human being: between what he grasps of the good, as the goal of humanity, in his enlightened moments, and what compels him from out of his own egotism, from his subconscious. It is not easy to recognize egotism in all its disguises, in its mask of altruism, of wanting to help, even of sacrifice. But weaknesses should be recognized as such, even if they represent themselves as strengths.

The process of self-knowledge consists in letting *both* of the warring parties within the soul speak out, in hearing and acknowledging both of them. Conscience is not fit for this task, because it was not formed by the *I*. The opposing side goes unnoticed when conscience "speaks," and so we never really come to terms with it.

From this point of view of self-knowledge we ask: what is going on out of egotism and what is contributing to goals worthy of mankind? Most of what I do has these two components. We can pay attention to what it is that helps or hinders us in the execution of the various exercises: this can orient us in relation to the opposing energies.

If we think through the exercises of the Eightfold Path, we notice that, aside from the exercise of right speech (described in detail) and the seventh exercise, these exercises make demands on the practitioner that cannot be instantly fulfilled. Even in the first exercise, the distinction of essential from unessential and of eternal from ephemeral is not easy. It is also difficult to decide whether a decision is correct (second exercise); to take on the viewpoint of humanity as a whole (fourth exercise); to live in accord with nature and the spirit (fifth exercise); to set oneself ideals that further the evolution of mankind (sixth exercise); to gauge how one stands in relation to the totality of humanity's goals (eighth exercise). All this is only possible through the slow, thorough learning and cultivation of a new worldview. But each exercise also contains points of departure from which anyone of good will can make a start. It is possible to restrict oneself to these parts of the descriptions. We have seen how far the exercise of right speech can lead. The exercises of the Eightfold Path —in contrast to the last four supplementary exercises—are limited to a specific time span, perhaps ten to thirty minutes.

It is evident that all the exercises presented here avoid direct involvement in the world of feeling. They create the space for a new, cognitive feeling to appear, for example, between thought concentration and will initiative. Finally, any of the given exercises can be deepened through meditation and carried further indefinitely.

Anyone who begins to do exercises of consciousness has to forget them when not actually exercising, so that life's spontaneity is not lost. A person who anxiously keeps to the rules, a person continually worried about his own physical and spiritual health, is not healthy. We need to *make an effort* to stay spontaneous—a ridiculous way of putting it, but it has to be said somehow. "Being worried" is an affair of the normal egotistical consciousness, and this alone shows that it must necessarily contradict the endeavor to school one's consciousness.

If exercises of consciousness are performed, then they will result in experiences. Doing the exercises and having *no* experiences means that something is being done that runs contrary to the given descriptions. It is fundamental to be able to distinguish between experiences of the soul and experiences of the spirit. At first this is not easy, because normally one has no idea what a spiritual experience is; one has no model for it and imagines something quite incorrect. This is why it is so important to have experience of living thinking —the spiritual experience nearest to hand. Once it has been experienced, we have a measure or model that enables us to make the necessary distinctions. Experiences of the soul are always self-feeling—one feels happiness or pain or a recognizable mood. Such experiences regularly occur in the course of the exercises, and their appearance does not of itself represent any error. The error comes about when these feelings are cultivated or when one turns one's attention toward them. Then they become distractions. The attention should *not* be directed to them, but toward the theme of the exercise. Spiritual experiences always point *away* from one's separate self, even when they are of the nature of feelings. Anyone who listens to music and relates it to his own being, to his own mood, achieves an experience of the soul. Anyone who directs his attention, not to the echo in his own soul, but to what the music itself is saying, and surrenders to *that*, has a spiritual experience. Spiritual feelings have a quality of their own, and they cannot be ranged along the axis that stretches from "good-for-me" to "bad-for-me."

What has just been said is especially important in the case of a generally applicable exercise that can be undertaken periodically (daily or weekly). It can be called *retrospection,* because the practitioner pictures to himself the experiences of the day or of the week in reverse order: the exercise begins with the last experience and ends with the first. The person should picture the experiences livingly, seeing his own figure as if from the outside. This backward mental picturing is not easy. It can be helpful at the start to picture only small portions of the day's story in reverse, and to then gradually take on longer stories. The exercise pursues several goals at once: self-knowledge, first, by regarding oneself as if a stranger. This is aided by the backward direction, which stimulates the habitual stance less than usual, even in regard to feelings, and furthers one's objectivity. Second, it exercises our capacity for mental picturing, releasing it from its accustomed paths. Picturing stories, events, or novels backward can be of help here.

The question now becomes how to set up a path of schooling. Because the task is individual, only the beginning, at most, can be suggested for the general case.

After the appropriate study (Section 5.2), a person can start with the concentration of thinking. After some time, the exercise of right speech is added, both of them at the appropriate level. These two exercises form the foundation of the path of schooling. If one has no success with the concentration of thought, then one tries a simple exercise in perception as a preliminary.

Later, another exercise from the six supplementary exercises can be added each month in alternation to the two basic exercises. The practitioner can read through one exercise per day from the Eightfold Path, contemplatively, slowly, and then try on the following day to pay attention to the corresponding processes in the soul, perhaps at a predetermined point in time. Concentration in mental picturing and in perception should definitely be added, but in such a way as to suit the individual's needs.

One begins to meditate when one's concentration has become sufficiently secure, otherwise the attempt leads inescapably to a dreamlike state that is of course the very opposite of meditation and can be characterized as a counterexercise if it happens regularly. Appropriate themes for meditation are those described in Section 5.3, but also, especially, the first fourteen verses of the Gospel according to John.

Anyone who lives into the practice of meditation finds his

own way by himself, both through his spiritual-scientific readings and in terms of his spiritual work and path.

Meditation is an advanced phase on the path. It leads us beyond the egotism that normally permeates our whole lives. It is, then, no longer a private affair, because it is the most individual activity. Therefore, it is fitting that this chapter should close with a meditation that relates to its place in the world process:

WHOEVER GIVES, RECEIVES.

6

ON HUMAN
FREEDOM

Why Speak of Freedom?

In Section 2.2 we said that a clock does not *know* what time
it is, even if it is a very complex computer clock. We know
this because the clock is constructed from materials that have
absolutely no similarity—neither in substance nor in function—with those that make up the human organism. But we
can imagine an even more fantastic apparatus, built from
nerve and brain tissue. Would it know the time? I hope that
every reader will now answer with a decisive "No." Whether
or not a knowing (human) consciousness is present does not
depend on the apparatus, which, even if it were infinitely
complex and built of the most suitable materials, would still
never be a "someone," a "who," an *I*. *This* principle, an *I*,
can express itself through a healthy human body just because
it is independent of this apparatus. And this principle reveals
itself in the phenomenon of the autonomous attention, which
is not based on physiology and has none. This principle is
free. How far and how continuously it can realize this freedom—a freedom of consciousness, a freedom of the atten-

215

tion—depends on the structure and inner forces of the soul.

To undertake measures appropriate to the health of consciousness presupposes a minimal freedom or autonomy: the reader can at least read the text attentively and understand it; he can at least try to apply the suggested measures, that is, he commands a minimal moral and cognitive freedom. Every halfway normal human being assumes this freedom and lives by it. But the usual "scientific" way of thinking, which is widespread, cannot come to terms with this idea of freedom because it lacks just this idea, the idea of the *I*. On the one hand we have force, mass, cause, atom, energy, and fields of force, and in that conceptual arena, *I*, friendship, morality, and freedom have no place. The subliminal conviction that man is completely unfree or predetermined, even in his consciousness, destroys the possibility of cognition and of moral action: truth and error, good and evil, have meaning only through freedom. It is also clear that human freedom has nothing to do with the indeterminability or unpredictability of physical processes: a chance event is not free. If I concentrate my attention on something, that is not a chance event.

If the self-evident feeling of freedom allows us to act, but the scientific way of thinking is unable to grasp freedom, then a contradiction lives in our consciousness that robs human decisions of their power and condemns us finally to a general laziness (to which we are prone in any case): If I am not free, then of course I can't do anything. The human being fails to notice the contradiction in this thought. And soul hygienic measures cannot be undertaken with the conviction that the human being is determined, which also makes it impossible to change one's attitude toward one's work or toward one's fellows. If man were determined, that is, unfree, even in his knowing, then he would not be able to know about this very circumstance. If he does have the possibility of freedom, but fails to realize it due to a scientific opinion about unfreedom, then he falls ill. If he discovers and practices his freedom in knowing, then this gradually radiates out through his actions. But he has to fight for his freedom on many fronts. Forgiving or reconciliation does not mean giving up without a struggle, and particularly not giving up one's inner freedom. It is not the purpose of the exercises in consciousness to make us complacently reconciled with *ourselves.*

In many of the soul's parts and members, the human being of today is already formed, molded, finished. His goal can only be to become more and more unfinished. But this can happen only by means of a *beginning:* through his autonomous decision and his actions, he himself begins to dissolve his already formed, habitual being. As soon as he begins, he receives help from his superconscious: the less the obstacle of the habitual man stands in the way of inspirations from above, the more the latter become new sources of power and orientation for him. In the phrases of Matthew 7:7, "Ask, and it shall be given you; seek, and ye shall find; knock, and it shall be opened unto you," the emphasis is on man's activity, man's beginning.

What is Freedom?

This question can best be answered by considering the opposite of freedom. When is something, a process, *not* free? When it follows necessarily from natural laws. In mechanics, in the mineral, plant, and animal kingdoms, laws of an "If . . . , then . . ." form apply strictly. If the temperature rises above 0° Centigrade, then ice begins to melt. If a bean falls to the earth, then it begins to grow after a certain time. When October comes, the deer begin to mate. In many human activities, we see the validity of such laws. But there are also human activities for which this is not always, not necessarily, the case. We cannot say: if the poet has slept well and had a good breakfast, then he will write the poem, "Tintern Abbey." We cannot say if he will write anything at all, much less how the poem will sound.

Just as little can we predict when someone will understand something: a discovery, a joke, the idea of an action, a question. Certainly, everything has its conditions. Only for a physicist can the swinging chandelier present a problem or the falling apple prompt a question. Many people, even many interested in physics, had seen objects swinging before Galileo, and many had seen falling fruit before Newton. What these thinkers achieved, for all humanity, does not *follow* from either the pendulum or the apple. The apple that gave Newton the idea of gravitation was certainly not the first that ever fell.

From this train of thought, on the one hand, it is clear that only a *someone,* an I-being, can make a beginning. In the sense of the previous explanations, it is the unfinished, the nonreactive, the Speaker within man that has this capacity. Only from an I-being can we expect a *beginning.* To begin, as meant here, is to create from out of the void: naturally, this has its conditions, but it does not follow from them.

On the other hand, we can say: creating, asking, knowing, are, according to the exposition of this book, like sparks or loans from the superconscious. How can we say then that it is a beginning on the part of man if it comes to him from a realm of which he is not conscious? The answer which a *contemporary* human being can give is the opposite of what Luther once had to say of himself: "Here I stand, I cannot do otherwise"—inspired by a superconscious religious conscience or belief. Modern man could say: "Here I stand, but I could also do otherwise." The superconscious does not compel him; *he,* at home in his past consciousness, must embrace his superconscious inspirations and affirm them. *He* must achieve or accept them in the first place. And all this generally against the strong countercurrent of the subconscious, which governs almost the whole of life. This difference is comprehensible because of the evolution of consciousness. Today we live in an age in which the collective or institutional societal concern with the newly free superconscious forces has given way to their management by each individual.

We could formulate man's situation as follows: today he is placed between the superconscious and the subconscious. From the latter he is reached by strong, insistent impulses; from the superconscious the inspirations grow ever more meager if he himself does nothing to clear their way. Still, he can choose. Since he can look at his own consciousness, nothing compels him—at least, not in this respect.

In man himself there arises a great disinclination for his potential freedom: a disinclination to take, all on himself, the responsibility for himself. Belief in authority, looking for spiritual leaders, for infallible wise men, initiates on whom to rely in every case, for every question; or for worldviews that, like materialism, reduce everything to a single principle: the belief that man is a natural being so that he cannot *begin,* the belief in inborn egotism. For unless they achieve the concept of the I-being, questions about causes will never reach a last cause; one can always push the question further. The last cause in the chain backward is the first—the first "mover" of Aristotle—and it is the original will of an I-being, capable of making a beginning: questions that aim beyond this beginning have no meaning. Why did Mozart compose his Haffner Symphony? Why did Schiller write the *Jungfrau von Orleans?* Why did X.Y., sacrificing his own life, save another person? You might say, "He wanted to. . . . " But why did he want to? The questions have to end there, as they could have at the first question, of which the last is merely a verbal variation.

If mankind asks about beginnings, origins, it must realize that a beginning is neither possible nor imaginable in the realm of the impersonal, the I-less. The questioner should ask himself the question, "Why am I asking questions?"

The Reality of Freedom

We feel free. We live, act, and speak as if we were silently convinced that we are free in our choices, decisions, and sacrifices. Often we fool ourselves, since we do not see through our own hidden, perhaps subconscious motives. Or, to the extent that we do see through them, we do not know why they should induce us to act, because they are rooted in the subconscious. But, here too, it is the past consciousness that decides. Free choice is endangered when associations, thoughtlike mental pictures crop up in our thinking. But as far as I am in a position to guide my attention, my thinking, mental-picturing, and perceiving attention, to *that* extent foreign motives that do not originate with myself will not coerce me. Can I think, observe, mentally picture, whatever I want to? How far? For how long? The instant we test our capacity for concentration, it gives the measure of our freedom.

We lead our lives as if man were free, and our penal law presupposes it, while recognizing circumstances that mitigate responsibility, such as drunkenness, psychological illness, and so on. But our *understanding* stands in contrast to the feeling of freedom and to the way we live. It has a hard time finding the possibility of freedom within the soul. The difficulty comes from not knowing the principle of the *I:* science and the general manner of thinking do not know the idea of this reality, which is the essence of man, although it alone makes possible every science, every doubt, every utterance. The following thoughts can help lead us to this idea.

When we speak about freedom and unfreedom, if we attribute any meaning, any truth value (or even falsity value) to this speaking—if we "attribute" anything at all—then this can only happen through freedom; otherwise our speaking about it would be a natural process, that is, predetermined. In that case, we would not even be able to tell that we were unfree, since even that assertion would be unfree—still, unfreedom could be the case. The feeling of freedom would be an illusion. But then the authority that notices this illusion, that recognizes it as illusion, would have to be free. Otherwise noticing and commenting would have no meaning.

"We *could* not notice it"; "Otherwise it *would* have no meaning." There is something in these sentences that cannot come about in a predetermined system such as nature or a computer: the conditional (the form of possibility), which is a gesture of the human soul. Predetermined systems can only make statements of the form, "A is the same as B." "Although," "also," "but," and so on, come from the human soul, like "silence," "peace," "beginning," and "end." Even a computer equipped with a randomizing function is predetermined—to be the way it is. The concepts mentioned above are among those that can only be grasped intuitively; they cannot be led up to or "explained." They have a source other than nature. We still feel this, powerfully, when a child uses words like "although," or "in earnest"; we listen closely, generally unconscious as to why: it is because these words originate in the private life of consciousness, and we are amazed that the child has come so far.

The source of these concepts lies in man's freedom. It only seems that perceptual objects need not be grasped with the same kind of intuition. *Where* an object ends can only be grasped by the conceptualizing intuition. *All of language, all of thinking, is possible only out of a sphere of freedom.* This is why there can be truth and error in thinking—*discovered* truth, of course, and *discovered* error.

We have practical experience of freedom of the will in, for example, the exercise on concentration. At first, being concentrated seems to be a *narrowing* of the attention, because we direct it to the theme and do not allow it to ramble every which way as usual. But the question arises: is a rambling attention really attention at all? And the narrowing is not merely the avoidance of other objects, but rather the concentration of an otherwise scattered force. Through this force— now focused on a single theme—our concentrating becomes not just an "omission" but an event of a different quality, on another plane normally untouched by consciousness. This activity occurs, as we said, out of freedom, and through it we experience the basic situation of the soul: the limitation of its freedom by means of distractions that stem from the subconscious: "I do that I would not."

This is where man's struggle for freedom, for the autonomy of his soul life, takes place. For freedom has nothing to do with external circumstances. These may be able to limit, hinder, even compel people as far as their behavior, the *exe-*

cution of their will, the realization of their intuitively grasped ideas for action. The fundamental question is whether in ourselves, in our consciousness, we are free. If not, then the problem of outer circumstances falls away. If we are free in our knowing and in our intentions, only then does the question of how to realize our freedom become real. If an appeal is made to circumstances as limiting or hindering one's freedom, then there is a tacit assumption that consciousness is free. Any other assumption leads to self-contradiction.

Speaking, thinking, or standing upright cannot be inherited. Children can acquire any language for their mother tongue with equal facility, independent of their family origin. Not even the capacity for vowel formation is inherited—otherwise children's pronunciation would give them away if they learned, as their mother tongue, a language other than that of their parents. Only something finished, already formed, can be inherited. In these capacities, therefore, man is free.

Inner freedom, freedom of consciousness, expresses itself in the modern capacity for asking questions, real questions. If these are not mere formalities ("What time is it?"), but aim at something truly essential, then they can only be present through freedom, or absent through lack of freedom. In a determined system, a *question* can have significance as a formality at most. Plants, animals, and machines do not ask questions. But for man, who is capable of asking questions, it is often difficult to pose the *right* question. This is always his biggest, weightiest question—always a question about the *meaning of the whole.*

Man *could* have an unbelievable amount to ask. We have seen that he stands in a different relation to nature than to the man-made world, because he does not know the meaning, the function, of natural objects and phenomena. He cannot think about them as penetratingly as he can a spoon or a hat. This means he could ask countless questions. His not doing so is the start of the renunciation of his own humanity, his failure, his abdication. To find these questions would require a healthy human understanding—a rarity of course, but still not impossible. To then pursue these questions would require a further freedom—not only will and work, but intuition. In any case: if someone has the will and works in this direction, he will also receive the necessary intuitions.

There is something only an I-being can have, because it is free and undetermined, and that is humor. In humor there is always some ambiguity, and humor can be understood only by someone who perceives the ambiguities *at the same moment;* who understands at the same moment the several meanings or possible interpretations of a situation or of a text. And these ambiguities are not predictable. In the problematics of computer science, the question is often asked as to whether and how a person could tell if he were talking with a human being or with a cleverly programmed computer. The simplest way to decide would be to slip a new joke into the conversation. If the words are taken seriously, and the joke goes unnoticed, then you know you are dealing with a computer, even if it looks like a human being. There are many people who cannot understand any jokes, and this shows that they are on the way to becoming machines.

From all this, it is possible neither to affirm nor to deny man's freedom, because the whole sphere of habits, along with the subconscious and the whole of our biology, work in a predetermined way on consciousness, which manifests its freedom, its autonomy, in thinking and in attention. *Whether he realizes or renounces his possible freedom depends on each human being.* How far he advances on the path of freedom lies in part with himself, in part with his circumstances into which, to be sure, he has fallen partly through his own choice, but also partly through external events, often of a collective kind (war, for example) which give new turns to his fate. One thing is certain: he can be free, he can realize his potential freedom, only if he leads his life actively and creatively.

Everyday life forms a tightly closed circle of things, tasks, needs, and events, which cause us to have little occasion to look outside: only death, birth, and *knowing* point and lead beyond this circle. Life certainly does not *force* us earnestly to occupy ourselves with these gates that lead beyond our accustomed sphere. It is just this gesture that lies within the human being's free choice.

What Can a Free Human Being Accomplish?

There is a great difference between feeling one's freedom and, besides feeling it, also being able to ground it in insight. Then there is the still further step of being able to *experience* freedom. This happens by means of the often mentioned I-experience in the *present* (Section 4.4); we can express the experience as a temporally and essentially extended spiritual presence: what normally flashes forth can now "remain."

If man is convinced of his possible freedom, then not only will he find courage, and the insight that something can be done for the health of consciousness, but also the "facts," particularly the facts of the soul, will become diagnoses rather than unconquerable natural laws. It is a valid and correct diagnosis to say that today's human being is powerfully determined by egotism. The conclusion to be drawn from this realization is not "This is how it is, this is how it must be, this is how it should remain," but rather "This is how it is, but it should be different," because we realize that things cannot go on much longer like this. Marxism is quite right about historical materialism, at least in regard to the last centuries: history and politics are influenced and directed by the economic interests and goals of groups of people. But this does not imply that we must or should pursue this kind of politics in the service of a group; rather that we should try to overcome this *currently* active principle.

Today, people work (with few exceptions) because they have to. And they work egotistically, as if they were working for themselves. But this is a mere appearance: in a society where division of labor is the rule, a worker of any class has an insignificant claim on the products of his or her labor. In practice we are working for other people. This fact contradicts our intention, and so work seems like coercion. Human work is always spiritual and mental work, even if done by a machine, in which case the machine is a product of spiritual work (and not merely in its construction). Because human work is always spiritual work (no animal can do human work, because animals lack hands and lack the appropriate intelligence), it always relates to a trust in good workmanship. Even if this is checked mechanically, then we have trust in the manufacturer and in the work by means of which the checking device was made. Finally, man comes upon man—even if business and the economy have been largely mechanized. When I pay for something at a cash register, it is after all a theoretical possibility that the cashier could hide my money and then claim that I had not given him any, or I could demand change back from a hundred dollar bill that I had never given.

Life would be much easier if we realized that we work for others, and they for us. Then work would be felt much less as coercion and much more as joy: I am doing something for others. If we trace back the origins of *social* labor, we find its source in religious worship: in the work of bringing sacrifices to the godhead. As far as ethnological discoveries permit conclusions about prehistorical times, this kind of work is and was done with joy. The neighborhood deity of today is to be found in our "neighbors," in other human beings: the speaking essence within them. And we can imagine that by overcoming the principle of egotism, which is really *simply a problem of trusting,* we could do our work, once again, as a sacrificial office for the nearest godhead, for our fellow man —and perform it, once again, with joy. This transformation is a matter of trust because everyone can say: "*I* would be happy to work for others as diligently as for myself, but what about all the swindlers out there who would profit from the work of others without doing anything themselves?" I'm sure that there would be such people. But there are now as well, only they are hidden, camouflaged. We cannot say in advance

225

what they would do if they didn't *have to,* in principle, but only *could.* Just think how this might function in a department of your place of work. Or even: go ahead and realize this mood in a small circle of your own choice. Economically speaking it costs nothing to change the prevailing mood. I am certain that, if you do, *much* will be changed. Remember the genie in the bottle: this transformation of the mood around us would be a fitting counterexperiment.

It is experience that makes holidays possible for a person and for mankind: experience of superhuman realities and beings. No holiday can be rationally introduced or organized: if it is, then subconscious instincts are being appealed to. If the holiday is to be real, the reality must be experienced during it; a holy reality, not an everyday reality. Such realities were mediated in former times by religious institutions, as was the whole conduct of life. Even today, churches often claim this leading role, which, however, is relevant for fewer and fewer people. Everything falls more and more within the individual's responsibility. This individual character makes the experience of a holiday, which is always a social event, very difficult. It is therefore a precondition for modern holidays that human beings meet together who have individual experience of a superhuman reality or who can at least guess at it as an experience on the boundaries of consciousness. This means that these people begin to have experiences in the direction of their superconscious abilities, and that behind these abilities (of thinking, of evidence, of being able to speak without conscious knowledge of grammar and vowel formation), they feel the superconscious, superhuman beings that are active and that express themselves through these abilities. For these are wordlike abilities that must have a personality at their source: even when an ordinary word is heard, we can be sure that it stems ultimately from an I-being. These are abilities of the *community:* there can be no private thinking or speaking. It is not human beings who "invented" these faculties or implanted them in mankind. A religious expression for them would be logos abilities. When they were implanted the forms of worship were organized in terms of a pedagogy from above to below: from the source of what was to be instilled toward the place where these abilities belonged. Today, because these abilities are in human possession, we must find our way on our own, and proceed on our own toward further development.

The pedagogy of early humanity was compulsory; it reached man without any effort on his part, just as he needed to do nothing (and did nothing) in order to find himself in the state of the consciousness-soul, which makes it possible to behold one's own consciousness and the functions of consciousness. This very possibility brings the direction from above to an end: now, everything that brings us further can only come to us through the consciousness that we ourselves control. Now, we must *seek* the intuitions that will guide us further: they are not simply given to us. Through the consciousness that has been achieved without our effort we ourselves must now find our teachings, the sources of the light of consciousness. This pedagogy will not come so far toward us as it once did, extending all the way into everyday life. The sign, the emblem, for this noncompulsory, merely exemplary "direction," which remains in the supersensible, active at the upper limits of consciousness, is the name of a spiritual being that was familiar to many peoples under various appellations: in Europe it was called the archangel Michael. According to tradition, this being is ever concerned with the fate of humanity and has forced the dragon, the enemy of mankind, from out of heaven and down onto earth. That means into the zone of human consciousness. We can ask: what help is it, why should it be of aid to mankind to be exposed to a hostile power in our conscious life? Apparently, this has to do with the generalization of subconscious formations, which we can date at about the Romantic period.

In Michael we can recognize the spirit of those tasks that lie before the humanity of today. We can understand him as the symbol of the superconscious sources of human spiritual abilities, which await man's conscious, willed approach. The superconscious world, the *sources* of consciousness, were freed by Michael from the word-hostile forces. They await mankind in purity, while, in our everyday consciousness, we are threatened by the dragon power of the subconscious. This new pedagogy from out of the superconscious *waits* for us; it does not come down to us of its own accord, does not influence us without our own effort. *That* is Michael's power —that he *waits*. His power consists in the power of those human beings who seek him; he expends it in such a way that it becomes their own power through which they seek and find him. This is why his power is that of mankind. Through experiences at the limits of consciousness, we can know about this power; it lies within our freedom to seek this source, to near it, to find it. Michael does not entice us. He is simply *there,* in the zone of wordless thinking, as the lord of language, standing wordlessly above all word languages as their original power. He has freed this zone from the dragon, so that the human being can attain (in wordless thinking) his inspirations—inspirations through which the everyday consciousness can be healed and the hostile subconscious forces can be conquered in earthly life.

The four seasons are adorned and consecrated with four holidays, as they were even in pre-Christian times. Winter brings Christmas; Spring brings Easter; Summer, St. John's day; Autumn, Michaelmas. The festival of St. Michael has barely any traditional content: it is for man to create it. This can only take place when there is a free gathering of striving individuals, not organized from the outside, who have chosen the inspiration of Michael as the goal of their efforts and who are in fact guided by this inspiration. The example of the dragon slayer gives them the power of conquering the dragon in themselves. Then the inner space becomes free and pure for the development of a new society and a new form of religious worship, now directed from below to above. From out of the first newly constituted holiday there will awaken the ability to enliven and to experience the other traditional holidays with a transformed content.

In Section 5.5, we discussed fate. It is a natural question to ask how fate and freedom can be combined in a single human being. To understand this, we must form a correct mental picture of fate.

From the whole content of this book, it is clear that man can never be finished; rather, it is part of his essential nature to be always under way. The paths toward realization of the individual possibilities in each case will, of course, be just as individual. One's individual situation on a path is characterized by the combination, the harmony or disharmony, of the individual superconsciousness, consciousness, and subconsciousness. The really individual abilities, through which the *I* articulates and expresses itself on earth, in a body, stem from the superconscious: we can only speak, think, and perceive individually, although speech, thought, and perception are superindividual world phenomena. They appear through the individual human being; he participates in them. Just as he "learns" superconsciously to speak and to think (i.e., he acquires the superconscious "how" of thinking as a capacity), in the same way his superconscious leads him to the opportunities that he needs on his way. These situations never coerce us; we can always choose *how* to make use of the opportunities. The situations are partly prepared for by the past, determined by the person's previous paths. Not all events and opportunities are of this kind, however. Events also take place for people that are determinative of one's future fate—in an even looser, broader sense, even more generously, so to speak, than plant species or animal behavior are determined. It is really more a question of a *style* than of concrete occurrences. Fate, accordingly, refers to high inspirations that appear as opportunities in life and which we handle like other inspirations: choosing, refusing, accepting, or changing. Just as a language does not limit a person in terms of thinking or fantasy, but rather teaches an independent grasp of the means of expression, for example, word formation, so too the language of fate is not restrictive, but shows us, if we pay attention, those places where an opportunity can be freely taken or avoided in order to pursue our path. Fate consists in large measure of selective attention:

therefore a situation can mean much to one person and yet mean little, or something quite different, to someone else. A particular human being can mean everything to one person, while someone else finds this incomprehensible.

And so there is no contradiction between freedom and fate. On the contrary, we can speak of human fate only when freedom is possible. Human deeds are almost always a combination of the free, glad powers that originate in the superconscious and that which comes from the unfree, natural, subconscious part. The ensemble of these generally unequal halves results in the unique human figure: we can look at it with pride, seeing how far humanity has come in its great individuals, in Buddha, Socrates, Dante; or with sadness, seeing how low humanity has sunk in its distractions, passions, and diseases of consciousness. But there is something touching about this human figure, as we look at it now in parting, for it is under way with possibilities toward both good and evil. It proceeds uncertainly, stumbling, falling back, rushing ahead, often without clearly seeing its path. And this is reflected in human deeds. As Rainer Maria Rilke says:

> Out of infinite yearnings arise
> finite deeds like delicate fountains
> that tremble and bend over too soon.
> But our glad powers, that otherwise
> keep themselves hidden from view,
> are revealed in these dancing tears.*

* from *Das Buch der Bilder* (1902).

Afterword

In Section 2.1 I said, commenting on the character of a general, collective disease of consciousness, that it cannot be recognized by anyone who suffers from the disease. I promised, though the reader has probably forgotten, to explain how I could discover and describe this disease.

Readers who did not skip Chapter 5 will at least be able to guess. I became able to write about diseases of consciousness by following a schooling of consciousness. My experiences on this path form the basis of Chapter 5. Everything in this book, in fact, is based on experience. And I am very interested in experiences that *you* will have or have already had. Please communicate with me through the publisher. I already send you heartfelt thanks and wish you every success with the exercises.